MUSIC by HEART

Paperless Songs for Evening Worship

A Collection of Songs from the New Music Project

CHURCH PUBLISHING
an imprint of
Church Publishing Incorporated, New York

Every effort has been made to trace the copyright owners of material included in this book. The author and publishers would be grateful if any omissions or inaccuracies in the acknowledgments could be brought to their attention for correction in any future edition.

Church Publishing Incorporated
445 Fifth Avenue
New York, New York 10016

www.churchpublishing.org

5 4 3 2 1

Singing from the Heart

by Donald Schell

What does singing 'by heart' mean to you? To me it immediately suggests singing something known by memory and loved. It's also a feeling. Songs we know by heart come to us in a distinct, recognizable way, their words and music seemingly flowing out of us, continuous, effortless, and whole. A crowd (church or secular) singing "Amazing Grace" know where they're going. You can feel the music has come to mean more than the words, and that the moment connects to something more universal. And when it's by heart there's also something fresh and new in the moment, though the song is familiar. The music we sing by heart we've learned whole. Our memory connects mind, heartbeat and breath. It makes us feel whole.

Before Gutenberg invented the printing press making broad literacy possible, most people learned music as people learn and make music today in rural Africa and other places where traditional music and culture continue. Traditional communities make music much as we do at a summer camp. The forms and strategies may differ a bit, but typically a leader calls out a phrase and people repeat it, or a leader starts the people singing a phrase and cues small changes in it—words or music, again leading by demonstration and the people learning by repetition. At its best (and we certainly hear this in African freedom songs) part-singing comes naturally because people listen attuned to traditional harmonizations, and as they hear the specific tonal structure of the melody they add harmony.

Learning something by ear asks us to listen for both memorable pattern and surprises. Even though we're encountering something we've never heard before, this kind of singing asks us to use our memory from the beginning. So we hear, grasp the whole as best we can, and anxiously (and excitedly) sing it together, testing and reinforcing our memory with each repetition. We're listening for melody, not individual notes from the beginning.

Such singing is immediately relational. Singers trust and follow the leader into music. It's a different cognitive activity from reading and uses different parts of our brain from reading and synthesizing notes to melody. In traditional singing we are collaborating with one another the moment we open our mouths, following a leader, yet taking initiative and supporting each other.

The process or learning music from words and notes on a page (which does take us to wonderful music, and eventually to music by heart) doesn't begin with hearing a melody or phrase, but in interpreting signs, working to combine them into a whole that won't emerge until we've followed each step, and so it's synthesizing note by note as we go waiting, eagerly (and impatiently) until symbols become sounds that reveal the phrase or melody.

Since the invention of the printing press, technology and media have shaped liturgy, and in the process have changed what we mean by liturgy. We're very aware of the benefits of that shaping. Printing and other technologies make planning and leading liturgy more complete and orderly, so in that way easier. Print can raise the quality of what we're trying to do. Printed directions, text, and music for everyone help readers learn music and keep together. Print media increases the range of what sources we can use. Print (like musical instruments) and sound systems amplify leaders and enhance the distinction between their authority and the authority of the rest of the congregation.

When we look at music on the page, we're looking at two different languages, each with its own symbol system. We're reading text (typically poetry when we're singing) where we recognize shapes from a phonetic alphabet, associate the shapes with sounds, choose options among the ways the sounds can be combined to make words (and phrases), combine some of those words into phrases. Meanwhile we're reading musical notes for melody or other voice part in the music. These symbols are a relational system, inherently different from a phonetic alphabet with multiple characters. Each note represents a relationally defined tone in a scale. For the "sense" of it, what matters is the relational place of the note in the scale. Simultaneously the notes tell us relational time value, again not in seconds, but in twice or half or whatever multiple or fraction of the length of adjacent notes.

People who enjoy reading music and are good at it can take pleasure in this multi-dimensional shape recognition,—simultaneous abstraction and synthesis in two different modes of thinking, and interpretation. It is a gloriously human, complex analytical and interpretative skill that takes singers and musicians from abstract symbols to the creation of beauty and expression of powerful feeling. In recent times the challenge of this double-reading system has also drawn a harder line between musicians and non-musicians, singers and non-singers. Self-described non-musicians and non-singers are generally people who can't sight-read. How do we get them to venture in? to begin singing? How does the church welcome their voices (and their music)? How can the church help them free the God-given music in their hearts?

Choral folk traditions bind the best singers and beginners together singing in one community. A solo singer offers a lead that welcomes other voices in by the flow of memory and repetition. All the singers discover pattern in text and music, helping them find their way to ownership of the congregational part or parts. Some may add improvisation. Perhaps the leader hands off that role to another leader.

These choral folk traditions teach a way of singing with the mind in the heart, learning directly by singing in a flow of memory and feelings.

People today still want to sing, even those (and maybe especially those) who call themselves "non-singers." Non-singers hope something could replace their shame at what they "can't do" with a freedom and renewed desire to sing—and where better than in church?

When much of the music we offer here was first composed and in development, I got to sing with the composers. We were literally singing new songs to the Lord morning and evening, and I don't think I've ever enjoyed singing so completely. That's the gift of this kind of singing. Singing by heart touches our desire to sing and by touching the deep places where music comes from, it renews and deepens our love of singing.

Since we began to develop it, I've used this musical approach and some of this music for workshop liturgies with clergy, church musicians, and laity. In the *Music that Makes Community* workshops, I've seen people leading and teaching music who had no idea they could do that. The summer camp likeness hints at the fun people have singing better than they knew they could. Teaching by heart and by ear makes learning music a grace for both leaders and congregation. It's possible, of course, to make a whole liturgy from this music. Or it may be something to add to a formal Sunday with choir, hymnals, and regular service music; a small invitation to include those who don't yet know they can sing.

But it also touches something deep and courageous in the Gospel itself. At the end of the Last Supper as Matthew tells it, just before Jesus went out to pray in the Garden of Gethsemane to face the conspiracy of Roman authority and some religious leaders to kill him, Jesus and the disciples sang a hymn (probably a psalm) together to celebrate God's power in the face of whatever was coming. (see Matthew 26:30) I can't imagine they had hymnals or paper music. Unless we sometimes sing our music by heart, there are times of great need when we'll have no music at all.

Singing Paperless Music in Your Congregation
A Practical Guide

Emily M. D. Scott

What is Paperless Music?

Paperless music is a way of singing that has been practiced in communities around the world since people have sung. It is a way of teaching and leading song without notes or words written on paper. Music is taught through call and response, patterns are established, and music making begins. This book is designed to help you begin to lead this type of music—simple, beautiful, tapping the depths of human experience—in your congregation.

Leading paperless music is different from directing a choir or accompanying a hymn, in that the skills and techniques are different. It takes practice and effort to learn these skills. Some of us will excel naturally, while others will need to work at it. However, the beauty of this style of singing is that it is born of community and practiced in communities. Most anyone who puts in the time and effort can learn to lead paperless music.

A Few Things to Think About

If you are a choral conductor, leading paperless music will require you to develop a second conducting style. Leading music by heart is not conducting. Congregants need you to help them learn the phrases of music you are teaching them through your gestures, to bring them in at the proper time, and to provide them with support when they falter. Much of this teaching and leadership may look very different from the conducting patterns you might use with your choir.

After some time leading this music, you will begin to develop your own style. Song leaders around the world have their own ways of leading groups of people in song. The techniques I've outlined here are just the beginning. Once you've mastered them, develop them and make them your own. Don't be afraid to try teaching the pieces in this book in a myriad of different ways. This is an oral culture, and as such is practiced differently in each community. Your church will find their own ways to sing these songs.

Remember that this music thrives on repetition. If you are a trained musician, you may be bored with music that is repeated again and again. This is not the experience of your congregants. They are luxuriating in the harmonies they are creating—an experience that might be entirely new to them! Let the music continue until the congregation tells you it is time for it to stop.

The most important element of this type of leadership is confidence. Your congregants will be secure in their learning and singing if they feel that you are 100% sure that they can do this. Leading this music the first few times may test your nerves. Remember to smile and give your congregation an encouraging look. If you're confident, they will be too.

Dive right in! Most of these pieces need no verbal introduction at all. Don't give your congregation the chance to get nervous! Sing a phrase and hold out your hand. They'll sing it right back before they knew what hit them. Your gestures matter. Your congregants are watching you for non-verbal cues. You'll learn how to ask them to repeat after you, how to cut off one group but keep a drone going, or how to build a crescendo, all with a non-verbal vocabulary. The skills are different from conducting, but just as complex.

Drop out when you're no longer needed. Your role is to teach the congregation, get them going, and then let them sing on their own. As soon as you feel that they're stable and secure, limit your leadership. Sit down in your seat and limit your cues. The congregation will be empowered to sing.

Forms of Paperless Music

There are five musical forms represented in this volume, and we've come up with our own vocabulary to describe each form. You'll see the form indicated at the top of each piece. Some composers have combined two or more of the forms listed here. When you first learn a piece, take apart the form first, so you understand how the piece is constructed.

Simple Melody

A simple melody is just that: a melody sung in unison by the congregation. These pieces rely on the beauty of the melody itself. They are often composed such that congregants and choir members are able to intuit the underlying harmonies and begin to improvise as they sing.

Echo

An echo is a piece in which a cantor sings a line, and the congregation sings it back.

Round

A round is a simple melody, sung by several groups of people, beginning at different times to create harmony.

Call and Response

A call and response piece is different from an echo piece. In call and response, the cantor sings a line (the call) and the congregants sing a line back that is different from the call. Some call and response pieces are made up of multiple calls, each with a different response.

Layered

A layered piece involves dividing the congregation into groups, teaching each group a line, then singing all the lines together. Often layered pieces are "built" from the bottom up, so that the congregants can hear the harmonies as they are created. Layered pieces sometimes feature a cantor singing a descant that floats above the harmonies of the congregation.

Techniques

Each piece in this volume includes step by step instructions to help you learn to lead your congregation in singing. In time, you'll be able to take a look at any piece and figure out how to "do it paperless." Until then, here are the building blocks you'll need to get started.

How to teach a piece phrase by phrase

Every piece in this book begins by teaching phrases to the congregation. Whether you're teaching a round or a call and response piece, your congregation needs to learn the musical phrases that make up the piece bit by bit. This is a simple but important process.

Indicating yourself, (I tend to place my hand palm down above my heart) sing the phrase you would like to teach clearly and strongly. Then, using a large gesture, have the congregation repeat the phrase. You'll have to experiment with what works for you in getting the congregation to repeat what you've taught them.

Many paperless song leaders use one hand to indicate the pitches in the melody they're teaching, to help the congregation learn. Flatten the palm of your leading hand, keep your wrist and forearm straight moving them up and down from the shoulder. Hold your hand out in front of your chest, parallel to the floor. The congregation will be seeing the edge of your hand and forearm. Now imagine that low notes are down in your belly button region, and high notes are near the top of your head. Moving your hand up and down along this spectrum in rhythm, you can show your congregation where the phrase is going, pitch-wise. Practice in front of the mirror to come up with a gesture that is clear but not rigid.

Be sure to teach the phrases in manageable chunks, one by one. Once the congregation has the small chunks down pat, sing the whole phrase, and have them sing it back to you. The congregation needs to feel secure with their parts before they can add harmony or do anything else more complicated.

How to divide a congregation into groups

Many of the pieces in this volume ask you to divide the congregation into groups. There are two simple ways to do this. The first is to simply say before your teach a line, "Low voices" or "High voices." When dividing the congregation into four parts, you could say, "Altos," or "Basses."

The second is to divide the congregation based on where they are sitting or standing in the space. This is particularly helpful when teaching rounds or layered pieces, because you can create as many groups as you need, and bring them in using gestures. It also helps create stability, because people singing the same part will automatically be seated together, and can depend on one another as they sing.

Create a group using only body language. Walk over to the group of people you'd like to sing first and face them, turning your back just slightly to the group who will not be singing. Sing the phrase you'd like them to learn. Then use your hands to clearly indicate that particular group, and make eye contact with the folks sitting in that section. Eye contact is key here, just as it is in conducting. Bring the group in on the phrase you've taught. Repeat this process with the next group.

How to encourage a pattern to continue

You may find that, after teaching a phrase, you would like the group singing it to repeat it, and then keep singing it as you bring in a second group on another part. One way to do this is to teach the phrase, cue the group to sing it again, and then gesture for them to keep going. I usually nod my head, raise my eyebrows, and move my hand in a circular pattern. Then stick around for a few moments to make sure the group has the idea. You don't want them to drift off when you turn around to work with the other group!

How to know when a piece is "established"

It's important to cultivate a sense of when a group is ready to sing a new part or descant, or to learn more. In this volume, you'll come across the phrase "established." We might say, "When the singing is established, bring in the duet." The secret to getting your singers established is to teach them well in the beginning stages. If they know their parts well, they will sing strongly, and the singing will become established quickly. If they are faltering as you teach them new material, it will be hard for them to gain confidence.

Listen to your group to see if they're established. They will fall into their own rhythm, be secure in their parts, and rely on one another for entrances, rather than on you. In the jazz world, we would say that they are "in the pocket." Be sure that your singing is established before you add another musical element.

How to end a piece

Just as you need to listen to your congregation to hear if they are secure in their singing, you must listen to them to know when it is time to stop singing. Allow an established piece to continue on its own, until you hear that you are reaching the last repetition. At this point, simply hold you hand up and give a minimal cut off. You don't have to give much. The congregation is ready to end the piece—they just need permission from you.

This may sound mystical, but it is the same unity of performance that occurs when a string quartet begins a piece, or when improvisers end a piece together. Your congregation is learning through the act of singing by heart to make music together as a community. At this point, it is not you who is leading the music, but the group. The congregation has become a body that breathes and sings together. They can decide when it is time for the singing to come to an end. You are there to hear that decision, and enable it.

Editor's Note

This book contains music that may be led in a congregation without the use of any books or photocopies, and mostly without rehearsing before hand. Congregants are able to sing from the heart and have their hands free to take part in worship: lighting candles, walking to the font—anything is possible. This volume is filled with pieces for evening worship. Many churches are beginning evening services for families or young people and are searching for musical resources. We hope this book will begin to fill that need, offering a variety of theologically rich pieces in a diversity of styles to be sung in the evening. You will also find numerous songs that could be used in worship at other times.

Many of these songs were composed during a retreat week sponsored by the All Saints Company and the Church of St. Gregory of Nyssa in San Francisco. During that week, composers prayed and sang together, discussed congregational singing, composed, and critiqued each other's work. The All Saints Company has also launched a series of conferences called "Music that Makes Community" to instruct people how to teach and sing in this way. For more information see www.allsaintscompany.com. Later, other composers were also invited to contribute music that could be sung paperless. Such diversity has given us a broad spectrum of word and music that represents the musical creativity flourishing in the church today. We are committed to communal song that naturally comes to our hearts and minds when needed for the rituals in our lives. Our goal is to offer quality song to fill that need whether it be for celebration, prayer, grief, renewal, meditation, or joy.

Marilyn Haskel, Editor

Robinson McClellan

This song can accompany a congregational dance.

FORM: Echo over a four-bar ostinato

LEVEL: Medium

LEARN TOGETHER:
- Divide the congregation into low and high voices.
- Teach lower voices (Group 2) the four bar ostinato:

- Rehearse the most difficult echo part (in Group 1) beginning in bar 16. Teach the repeated figure, then show how the two figures overlap by bringing the congregation in with your hands, or giving verbal instruction.

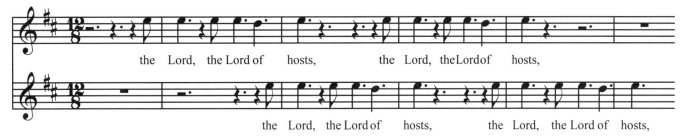

SING TOGETHER:
- Bring in the ostinato.
- Begin the echo.
- Repeat sections (at repeat signs) or the entire piece as desired.

Music follows on next page.

1 **Lift up your heads/Who Is This King of Glory**

Music continues on next page.

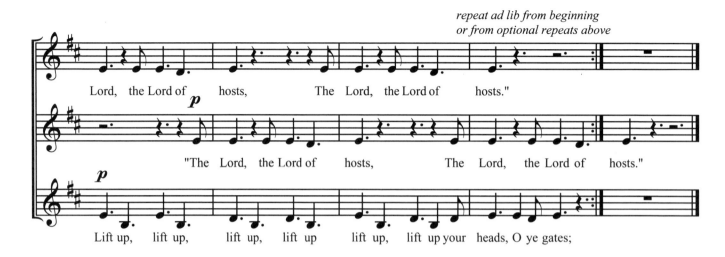

Words: Psalm 24:7-10.

Music: Robinson McClellan, inspired by the Welsh harp manuscript of Robert ap Huw (1623) © 2007 by Robinson McClellan, [www.robinsonmcclellan.com]. Used by permission. *This piece is also available as an anthem at the website listed.*

Robinson McClellan

This refrain may be used as a response for any chanted text, such as a psalm.

FORM: Call and response

LEVEL: Difficult

LEARN TOGETHER:
- Teach the first response.

- Sing the first call, invite congregation to sing first response.

- Teach the second response.

- Sing the second call, invite congregation to sing second response.

- Teach the monotone "Alleluia."

2 Alleluia

Sɪɴɢ Tᴏɢᴇᴛʜᴇʀ:
- Perform the first and second call and response.
- Lead the monotone "Alleluia" with everyone.
- Sing the cantor line over the monotone "Alleluia."
- Give a cutoff at the end of the monotone "Alleluia" and repeat as desired.

Music: Robinson McClellan, © 2007 by Robinson McClellan, [www.robinsonmcclellan.com]. Used by permission.
This piece is also available in an anthem setting at the website above.

Robinson McClellan

This piece makes use of two melodic patterns, one ascending and the other descending. Begin the phrases in metered time, and switch to speech rhythm at the double bar. Notice that in some phrases, the congregation is directed to sing together, rather than in an echo. Ask another cantor to lead the echo to give the congregation support as they sing.

FORM: layered echo, over drone

LEVEL: Difficult

LEARN TOGETHER:
- Bring in a drone on the tonic [C]
- Teach the whole piece, phrase by phrase, modeling the metered and free rhythms

SING TOGETHER:
- Divide the congregation into two groups
- Bring in the first group. The second cantor bringing in the second group.
- Conduct the rhythmic unisons together

Music follows on next page.

Words: The Book of Common Prayer (1979)
Music: Robinson McClellan, © 2007 Robinson McClellan, [www.robinsonmcclellan.com]. Used by permission.

Form: Echo with monotone echo

Level: Medium

Learn Together:
- Divide the congregation into two groups, one consisting of mostly high voices, the other mostly low.
- Say, "This piece has a monotone echo. Group 1 will repeat what I sing, but on one note that doesn't change. Group 2 will repeat exactly what I sing. Let's try that."
- Teach first phrase in monotone to first group.

- Teach first phrase with pitches to second group.

- Sing both groups together.

Sing Together:
- Continue piece, directing each group with one hand.
- Indicate with hand the pitch change on the last note in the monotone part.

Music follows on next page.

4   **Holy, holy, holy God/Sanctus & Benedictus**

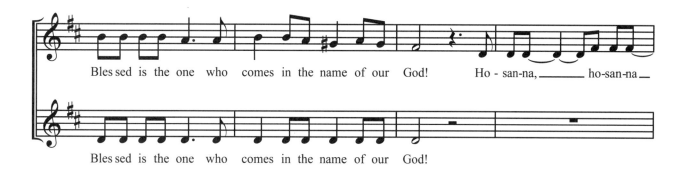

Bles sed is the one who comes in the name of our God! Ho - san-na, _____ ho-san-na _

Bles sed is the one who comes in the name of our God!

_ in the high - est! Ho san-na, _____ ho-san-na _____ in the high - est!

Ho - san-na, _____ ho-san-na _____ in the high - est!

Music: Robinson McClellan, © 2007 Robinson McClellan, [www.robinsonmcclellan.com]. Used by permission.

5 **Christ has died/Memorial Acclamation**

Robinson McClellan

FORM: Echo with monotone echo

LEVEL: Medium

LEARN TOGETHER:
- Divide the congregation into two groups, one consisting of mostly high voices, the other mostly low.
- Say, "This piece has a monotone echo. Group 1 will repeat what I sing, but on one note that doesn't change. Group 2 will repeat exactly what I sing. Let's try that."

SING TOGETHER:
- Continue piece, directing each group with one hand.
- Indicate with hand the pitch change on the last note in the monotone part.

Music: Robinson McClellan, © 2007 Robinson McClellan [www.robinsonmcclellan.com]. Used by permission.

Robinson McClellan

FORM: Echo

LEVEL: Easy

LEARN AND SING TOGETHER:
- Sing the first phrase, bring the congregation in on the echo.
- Continue on in this manner.

Music continues on next page.

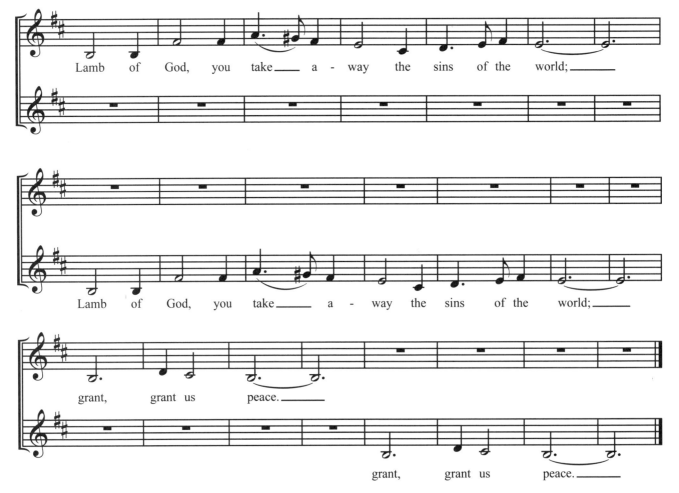

Lamb of God, you take a - way the sins of the world;

Lamb of God, you take a - way the sins of the world;

grant, grant us peace.

grant, grant us peace.

Music: Robinson McClellan, © 2007 Robinson McClellan, [www.robinsonmcclellan.com]. Used by permission.

This hymn was originally written in English, but is used in Gaelic translation by the Church of St. Columba in Glasgow. The composer has used the Gaelic only in the refrain which may be sung in either English or Gaelic. The pronunciation is printed in italics.

FORM: Call with layered response

LEVEL: Easy

LEARN TOGETHER:
- Divide the congregation into three groups.
- Teach the response to everyone:

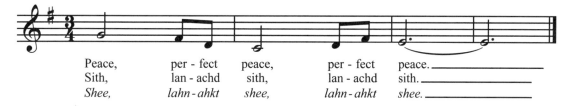

- Teach everyone the layered response.

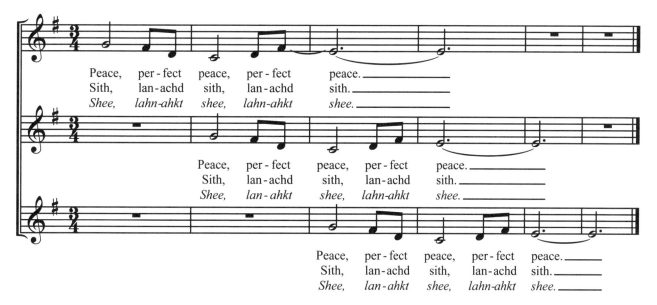

SING TOGETHER:
- Sing the cantor verse.
- Bring in the layered responses.
- Continue with additional verses.

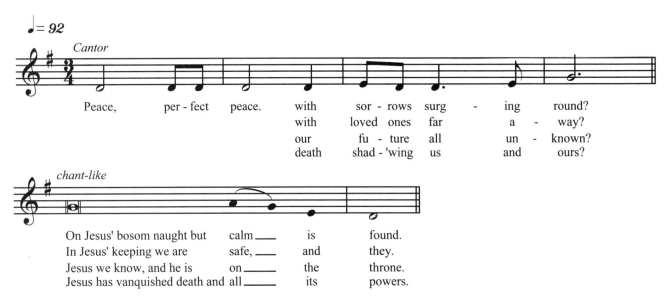

Words: Edward H. Bickersteth, Jr. (1875)
Music: Robinson McClellan, © 2007 Robinson McClellan, [www.robinsonmcclellan.com]. Used by permission.

Robinson McClellan

This setting of the Lord's Prayer is based on a rarely-heard type of Gaelic bagpipe music called pibroch which flourished in the 17th and 18th century Highland clan life.

FORM: Echo with monotone echo

LEVEL: Medium

LEARN TOGETHER:
- Divide the congregation into two groups, one consisting mostly of high voices, the other mostly low.
- Say, "This piece has a monotone echo. Group 1 will repeat what I sing, but on one note that doesn't change. Group 2 will repeat exactly what I sing. Let's try that."
- Teach first phrase of the prayer in monotone to Group 1. Note: the clear notes are to indicate reciting notes that are required for multiple words in subsequent verses. Teach the first phrase in speech rhythm, i.e., do not elongate "in" or "-lowed."

- Teach the first phrase with pitches to Group 2.

- Both Groups sing together.

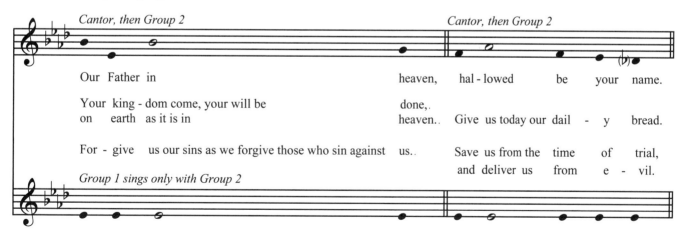

• Teach the final part for the drone echo of Group 1 noting where their drone pitch changes

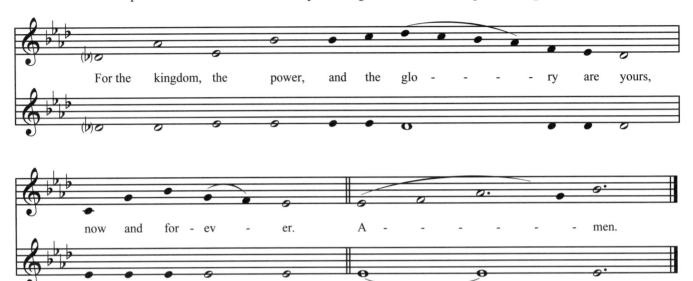

For the   kingdom,   the   power,   and   the   glo - - - - ry   are   yours,

now   and   for - ev - er.   A - - - - - - men.

• Teach the first line of the final section melody to Group 2.
• Both Groups sing together. Repeat several times.

SING TOGETHER:

- Continue piece, directing each group with one hand.

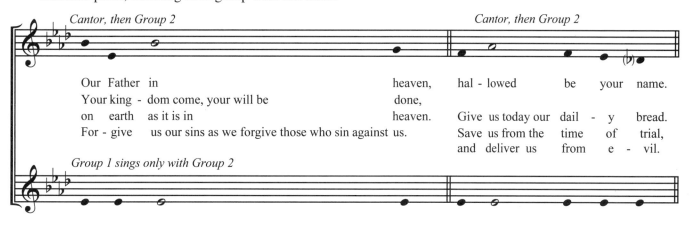

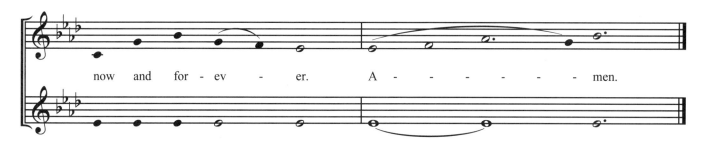

Words: Book of Common Prayer
Music: Robinson McClellan © 2007 by Robinson McClellan, [www.robinsonmcclellan.com]. Used by permission.

9 Send your light forth

Robinson McClellan

The tricky rhythms of this chant may be supported by a drum or hand clap. The piece should be sung with a steady beat and plain expression – each syllable receives the same weight.

FORM: simple song

LEVEL: Difficult

LEARN TOGETHER:
- Divide the congregation into two groups, one consisting mostly of high voices, the other mostly low.
- Have them repeat the words once through.
- Teach the words in rhythm.
- Teach the first part phrase by phrase.
- Teach the second part phrase by phrase.

SING TOGETHER:
- Sing both parts together and repeat as desired.

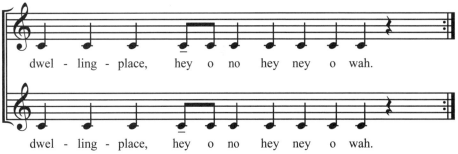

As the dark awaits the dawn   **10**

Frederick Frahm

Sing this piece as you light the lamps for an evening service.

FORM: Overlapping Echo

LEVEL: Easy

LEARN TOGETHER:
- Teach each repeated phrase in the first verse with no rhythmic overlap:

- Sing again with the phrases overlapped.

SING TOGETHER:
- Bring in the bell ostinato.
- Sing the first phrase and bring in congregation on the downbeat.
- Additional verses may be taught each week.

Music follows on next page.

night,
lease,
ness,

lov - ing bright, lov - ing bright,
liv - ing peace, liv - ing peace,
bright and blest, bright and blest,

Star of Pro - mise, scat - ter night,
let your heal - ing light re - lease,
through us stream your hol - i - ness,

lov - ing bright, lov - ing
liv - ing peace, liv - ing
bright and blest, bright and

till shades of fear are gone.
un - to your ho - ly dawn.
come dawn, O Sun of grace.

bright,
peace,
blest,

till shades of fear are gone.
un - to your ho - ly dawn.
come dawn, O Sun of grace.

Words: Susan Palo Cherwien, from *O Blessed Spring*, © 1997 Augsburg Fortress Publishers. Used by permission.
Music: Frederick Frahm, ASCAP, © 2007 by Frederick Frahm. Used by permission.

11   I'm walking with my God today

Nick Page

The small notes for harmony in the congregation part may be improvised.

FORM: Echo

LEVEL: Easy

LEARN TOGETHER:
  • Practice layered echo in measure 13 teaching it first by echo with no overlap, then as printed:

SING TOGETHER:
  • Sing the piece phrase by phrase, directing the congregation to repeat after you.
  • Give added support through gestures when you reach bar 13.

Words and Music: Nick Page, © 2007 by Nick Page. Used by permission.

12 All shall be well

William Bradley Roberts

This refrain works well sung between the phrases of a sung or spoken prayer.
Alternatively a cantor may read prayers or improvise on verses of psalms between repetitions of the refrain.

FORM: Drone with refrain

LEVEL: Easy

LEARN AND SING TOGETHER:
- Hum the notes of the drone, direct the congregation to hum with you.
- Indicate that the drone should continue.
- Teach the refrain and have the congregation echo it above the drone.
- Bring the congregation in together on the refrain.

Words: Julian of Norwich, (ca. 1342-1413)
Music: William Bradley Roberts, © 2006 by William Bradley Roberts. Used by permission.

William Bradley Roberts

A cantor may read prayers or improvise on verses of psalms between repetitions of the refrain.

FORM: Drone with refrain

LEVEL: Easy

LEARN AND SING TOGETHER:
- Hum the notes of the drone; direct the congregation to hum with you.
- Indicate that the drone should continue.
- Teach the refrain and have the congregation repeat it.
- Bring the congregation in on the refrain above the drone.

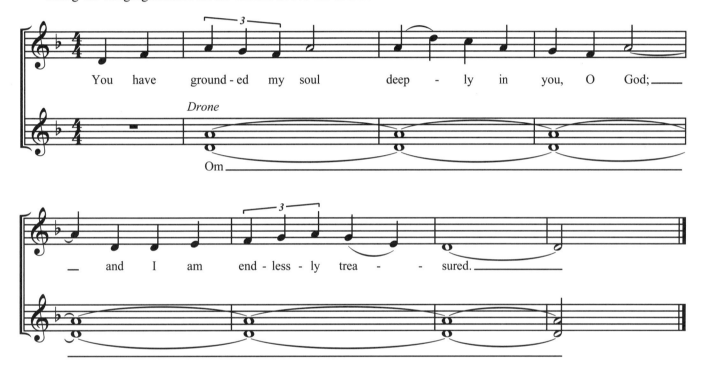

Words: Julian of Norwich (ca. 1342-1413)
Music: William Bradley Roberts, © 1995 William Bradley Roberts. Used by permission.

14   Let the broken ones be healed

Sandra Gay

FORM: Round

LEVEL: Easy

LEARN AND SING TOGETHER:
• Teach the round phrase by phrase.
• Sing the whole round through.
• Divide the congregation into three groups.
• Sing the round with Group 2 beginning when Group 1 reaches letter B, and so with C.

Let the brok-en ones be healed. Let the lost be found and fed. Let the grace of God roll on. Let the

ri - ver rise and spread. Step in - to the stream with me. Let God's gra-cious pur-pose be!

Eric H. F. Law

FORM: Round with cantor

LEVEL: Easy

LEARN TOGETHER:
- Begin by practicing bars 9-12:

- Teach the round phrase by phrase

SING TOGETHER:
- Divide the congregation into four groups
- Sing the round with Group 2 beginning when Group 1 reaches letter B, and so with C and D.
- When the round is established, bring in the cantor part being sung simultaneously.

Round

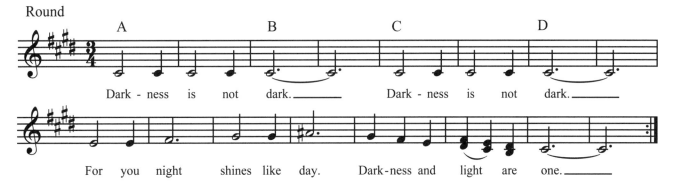

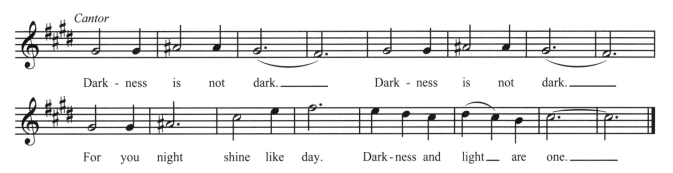

Words: Psalm 139:11
Music: Eric H. F. Law, © 2007 by Eric H. F. Law. Used by permission.

16   Let my prayer be set forth

Eric H. F. Law

Sing this piece as a response during meditative prayer in the evening.

FORM: Simple melody

LEVEL: Easy

LEARN AND SING TOGETHER:
- Teach the melody phrase by phrase.
- Sing the whole melody through.
- Add finger cymbals.

Words: Psalm 141:2
Music: Eric H.F. Law, © 2007 by Eric H.F. Law. Used by permission.

Eric H. F. Law

This round works well as an offering is presented.

FORM: Round with ostinato

LEVEL: Medium

LEARN TOGETHER:
- Teach the ostinato to the low voices.
- Teach the words of the round.
- Teach the round phrase by phrase.
- Sing the whole round.

SING TOGETHER:
- Bring in the ostinato.
- Divide the rest of the congregation into two groups.
- Sing the round with Group 2 beginning when Group 1 reaches letter B.
- Continue to cue the round entrances.

Round

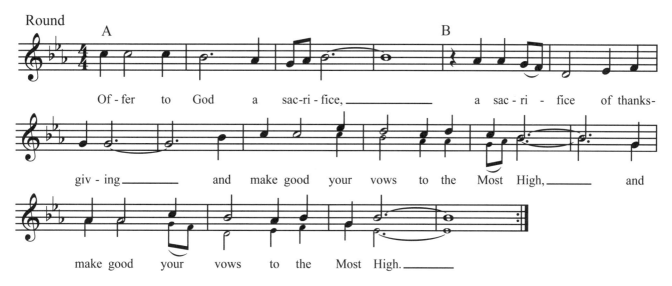

Of-fer to God a sac-ri-fice, _____ a sac-ri-fice of thanks-

giv-ing_____ and make good your vows to the Most High, _____ and

make good your vows to the Most High. _____

Ostinato

Of-fer to God, __ of-fer to God ___ a sac-ri-fice ___ of thanks-giv-ing. __

Words: Psalm 50:14
Music: Eric H.F. Law, © 1986 by Eric H. F. Law. Used by permission.

18   In God's image I was created

Eric H.F. Law

The rests at the end of the melody are necessary for the alignment of the four parts of the round. Give your congregation support on each round entrance so they don't become lost.

FORM: Round

LEVEL: Easy

LEARN AND SING TOGETHER:
- Teach the round phrase by phrase.
- Sing the whole round melody.
- Divide the congregation into two parts.
- Bring the parts in one by one.
- Continue to cue the round entrances.

- If desired, try the round in four parts

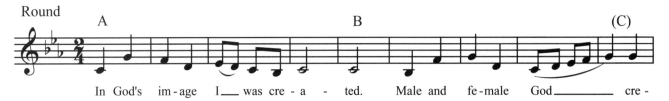

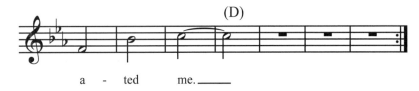

Words: Genesis 1:27
Music: Eric H.F. Law, © 1988 by Eric H.F. Law. Used by permission.

Eric H.F. Law

FORM: Round with ostinato

LEVEL: Medium

LEARN TOGETHER:
- Teach the round phrase by phrase.
- Sing the whole round melody.
- Teach the ostinato.

SING TOGETHER:
- Bring in the drum (optional).
- Bring in the ostinato.
- Bring in the melody line and sing through a few times.
- Divide the congregation in two parts and sing as a round.
- Continue to cue the round entrances.

Ostinato

Round

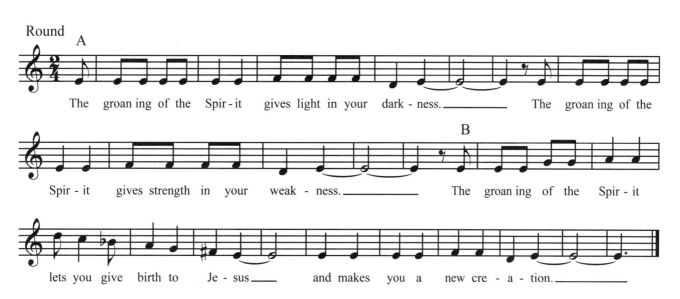

Words: based on Romans 8:14-27
Music: Eric H.F. Law, © 1988 by Eric H.F. Law. Used by permission.

Drum

20   Love your enemies

Eric H.F. Law

FORM: Round with cantor

LEVEL: Medium

LEARN AND SING TOGETHER:
- Teach the round phrase by phrase.
- Sing the whole round melody.
- Divide the congregation into three groups.
- Bring the parts in one by one.
- Continue to cue the round entrances.
- When the round is established, bring in the cantor.

- If desired, assign three cantors to sing the cantor line as a round.

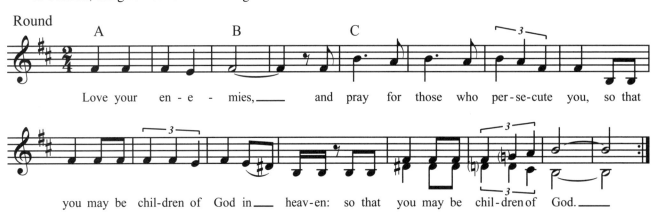

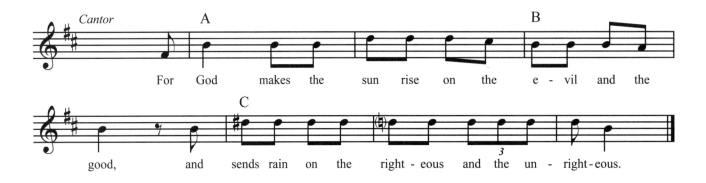

Words: Matthew 5:44
Music: Eric H.F. Law, © 1991 by Eric H.F. Law. Used by permission.

Eric H.F. Law

FORM: Round with cantor

LEVEL: Medium

LEARN AND SING TOGETHER:
- Teach the round phrase by phrase.
- Sing the whole round melody.
- Divide the congregation into three groups.
- Sing the round with Group 2 beginning when Group 1 reaches letter B, and so with C.
- Continue to cue the round entrances.
- When the round is established, bring in the cantor.

Words and music: Eric H.F. Law, © 1986 by Eric H.F. Law. Used by permission.

22   Jesu, Jesu, Jesu/Child of Mary

Eric H.F. Law

FORM: Layered

LEVEL: Medium

OPTION 1

LEARN TOGETHER:
- Divide the congregation into four groups.
- Teach Part 1 phrase by phrase.

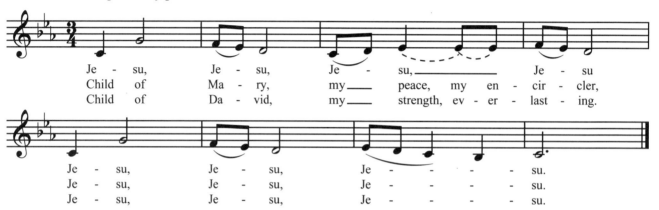

- Teach Part 2 phrase by phrase.

- Teach Part 3 phrase by phrase.

- Teach Part 4 phrase by phrase.

SING TOGETHER:
- Bring in each part progressively.

OPTION 2

LEARN AND SING TOGETHER:
- Teach Part 1 phrase by phrase.
- Sing the whole melody.
- Bring in cantors on Parts 2, 3 and 4 progressively.

Words and Music: Eric H.F. Law, © 1988 by Eric H.F. Law. Used by permission.

23 Lord have mercy/Confession

Isaac Everett and j. Snodgrass

FORM: Layered with cantor

LEVEL: Easy

LEARN AND SING TOGETHER:
- Divide the congregation into two groups.
- Teach Part 1 phrase by phrase.

- Teach Part 2 phrase by phrase.

- Sing the two parts together.
- When the piece is established, bring in the cantor.

Music contiues on next page.

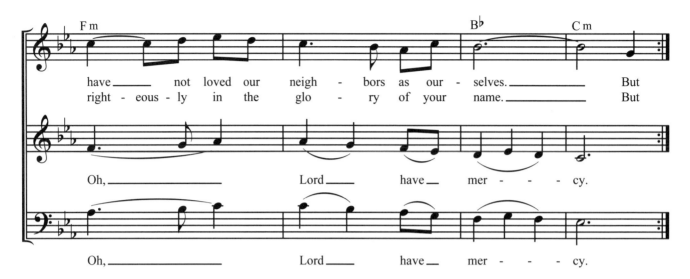

have_____ not loved our neigh - bors as our - selves._____ But
right - eous - ly in the glo - ry of your name._____ But

Oh,_____ Lord_____ have_____ mer - - - cy.

Oh,_____ Lord_____ have_____ mer - - - cy.

FORM: Round

LEVEL: Easy

LEARN AND SING TOGETHER:
- Teach the round phrase by phrase.
- Sing the whole round through.
- Divide the congregation into three groups.
- Sing the round with Group 2 beginning when Group 1 reaches letter B, and so with C.

Round

I asked my__ sa - vior, "Take me with you please, up to a world of

right-eous-ness and peace." And he__ ans-wered me, "Take me with you please_____

out to a world of right - eous - ness and peace."

Words and music: Isaac Everett and j.Snodgrass, © 2007 Isaac Everett and j.Snodgrass. Used by permission.

25   Kol hanneshama
Ana Hernández

"Kol hanneshama tehallel yah halelu-yah" is the last verse of Psalm 150 in Hebrew, and translates, "Let everything that has breath praise God." The words are pronounced as: Kohl-hah-neh-shah-mah hah-leh-yah hah-leh-loo-yah. This song is wonderful with percussion, and works as an Alleluia, Gospel Acclamation, Benediction, or at any other time!

FORM: Simple Melody

LEVEL: Medium

LEARN TOGETHER:
- Teach the words.
- Teach the melody phrase by phrase.
- Sing the whole melody.

SING TOGETHER:
- Sing the melody through.
- When the melody is established, try layering the sections.

Words: Psalm 150:6
Music: Ana Hernández, © 2007 by Ana Hernández. Used by permission.

FORM: Layered

LEVEL: Easy

LEARN TOGETHER:
- Divide the congregation into two groups.
- Teach the drone:

Yours the day al - so the night, you made the moon and the sun.
La la la la la la la la la la la la la la
God has bless'd us, God has bless'd us, let us bless_____ God. _____

- Teach the words to the melody.
- Teach the melody.

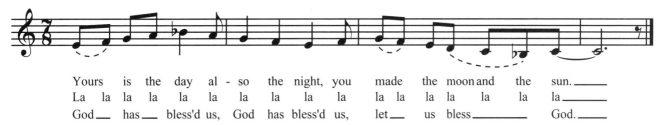

Yours is the day al - so the night, you made the moon and the sun. _____
La la la la la la la la la la la la la la la la la _____
God_ has_ bless'd us, God has bless'd us, let_ us bless_____ God. _____

- Sing both parts together.

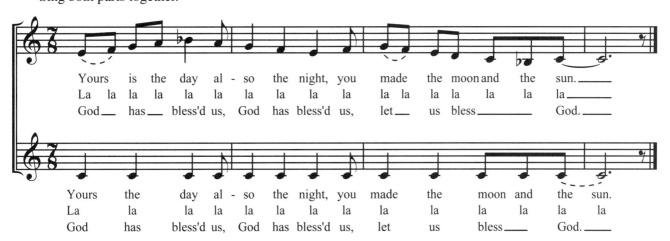

Yours is the day al - so the night, you made the moon and the sun. _____
La la la la la la la la la la la la la la la _____
God_ has_ bless'd us, God has bless'd us, let_ us bless_____ God. _____

Yours the day al - so the night, you made the moon and the sun.
La la la la la la la la la la la la la la
God has bless'd us, God has bless'd us, let us bless_____ God. _____

Words: Antiphon for Psalm 134
Music: Ana Hernández, © 2007 by Ana Hernández. Used by permission.

SING TOGETHER:

• Bring in the percussion as desired.

• Bring in the parts one by one.
• When the singing is established, call out the additional verses.

Additional verses

Come—	and——	bless	our	God	la	la	la	la	la	la	la	la	la	la——
You—	who——	stand	by	night	la	la	la	la	la	la	la	la	la	la——
In	this	ho - ly	place	la	la	la	la	la	la	la	la	la	la	la——
Lift —	up	your	hands	la	la	la	la	la	la	la	la	la	la	la——

Ana Hernández

FORM: Simple melody with cantor

LEVEL: Easy

LEARN AND SING TOGETHER:
- Teach the melody phase by phrase.
- Sing the whole melody.
- When the singing is established, bring in the descant sung by a cantor.

* *no thing* rather than *nothing*

Words: Angelus Silesius (1624-1677), tr. by Stephen Mitchell.
Music: Ana Hernández, © 2006 by Ana Hernández. Used by permission.

28 Evening lamps are lit/Firelight Praise

Ana Hernández

FORM: Layered

LEVEL: Easy

LEARN TOGETHER:
- Divide the congregation into two groups.
- Teach Part 2 phrase by phrase.

Light of the world, of end - less bless - ing, sun of our night, lamp of our days.

Light of the world, of end - less bless - ing, we raise our hearts in light and praise.

- Teach Part 1 phrase by phrase.

Eve - ning lamps are lit, fire - light all a - round.

Eve - ning lamps are lit, praise the on - ly sound.

SING TOGETHER:
- Bring in Part 2, then add Part 1.
- Bring in the drum, if desired.

Part 1

Eve - ning lamps are lit, fire - light all a - round._____

Part 2

Light of the world,___ of end - less bless - ing, sun of our night, lamp of our days.

Eve - - ning lamps are lit, praise___ the on - ly sound.

Light of the world,___ of end - less bless - ing, we raise our hearts in light and praise.

Words and Music: Ana Hernández, © 2006 by Ana Hernández. Used by permission.

Drum

29   If in your heart (First setting)

Ana Hernández

FORM: Simple melody

LEVEL: Easy

LEARN AND SING TOGETHER:
- Teach the words phrase by phrase.
- Teach the melody phrase by phrase.
- Sing the whole melody.

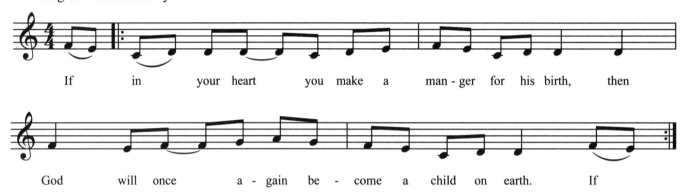

If   in   your heart   you make a   man - ger for his birth,   then

God   will once   a - gain be - come a   child on earth.   If

Words: Angelus Silesius (1624-1677), tr. by Stephen Mitchell.
Music: Ana Hernández, © 2007 by Ana Hernández. Used by permission.

- If desired, teach the clapping pattern by asking your congregation to clap twice, then move their hands outward to feel the eighth rest.
- When the melody is established, bring in the clapping. Notice that the clapping should be like a heartbeat with two claps always separated by an eighth rest.
- It may be helpful to have a drum with a steady pulse on beats 1 and 3.

Clapping

etc.

If in your heart (Second setting)　　30

Ana Hernández

FORM: Simple melody

LEVEL: Easy

LEARN TOGETHER:
- Teach the melody phrase by phrase.
- Sing the whole melody through.
- Begin to improvise harmony parts – the congregation will follow your lead!

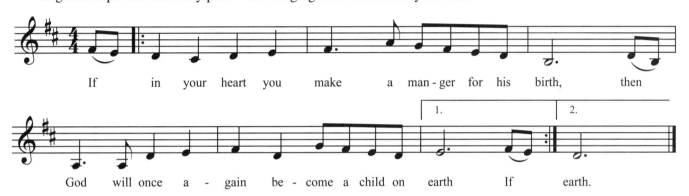

Words: Angelus Silesius (1624-1677), tr. by Stephen Mitchell.
Music: Ana Hernández, © 2007 by Ana Hernández. Used by permission.

31   Open my heart

Ana Hernández

This song may be sung before the reading of scripture or during communion.

FORM: Layered

LEVEL: Easy

LEARN TOGETHER:
- Divide your congregation into three groups.
- Teach Part 1.

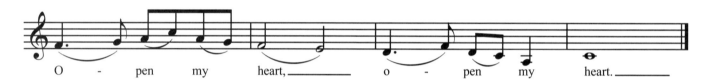

- Teach Part 2.

- Teach Part 3.

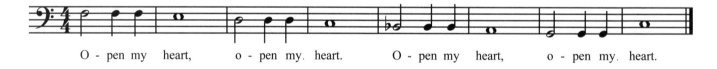

Sing Together:
- Bring in each part one by one.

Words: Ana Hernández, adapt. from a trad. Chinese mantra to the Buddhist goddess of compassion, Guan Shi Yin.
Music: Ana Hernández, © 2007 by Ana Hernández. Used by permission.

32　Where I go in the world

Ana Hernández

This Gaelic text comes from the Céile Dé, a Celtic Christian order.

FORM:　Layered

LEVEL:　Medium

LEARN TOGETHER:
• Teach Part 4.

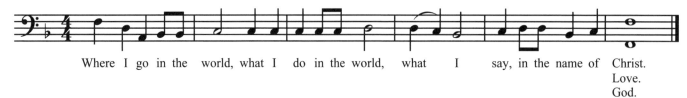

Where I go in the world, what I do in the world, what　I　say, in the name of　Christ.
Love.
God.

• Teach Part 3.

Where I　go　in the　world, what I　do in the world, what I say in the　world, in the name of　Christ.
Love.
God.

• Teach Part 2.

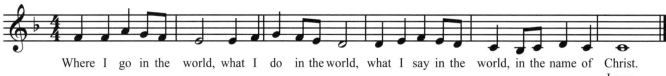

Where I　go　in the　world, what I　do　in the world, what I say in the　world, in the name of　Christ.
Love.
God.

• Teach Part 1.

Where I　go　in the　world, what I　do in the world,　what I say in the　world, in the name of　Christ.
Love.
God.

SING TOGETHER:
- Bring in each part, in the order you taught them.

Where I go in the world, what I do in the world,

Where I go in the world, what I do in the world,

Where I go in the world, what I do in the world,

Where I go in the world, what I do in the world,

what I say in the world, in the name of Christ. Love. God.

what I say in the world, in the name of Christ. Love. God.

what I say in the world, in the name of Christ. Love. God.

what I say, in the name of Christ. Love. God.

Words: Celtic chant of the Céile Dé order, alt.
Music: Ana Hernández, © 2006 by Ana Hernández. Used by permission.

33 Now daylight fades

Marilyn Haskel

FORM: Round

LEVEL: Easy

LEARN AND SING TOGETHER:
- Teach the words phrase by phrase.
- Teach the melody phase by phrase.
- Sing the whole melody.
- Divide the congregation into four groups.
- Bring in the groups one by one.

Round

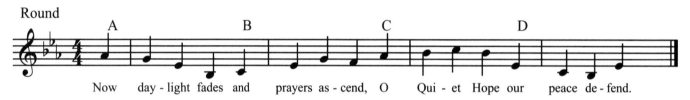

Now day - light fades and prayers as - cend, O Qui - et Hope our peace de - fend.

Words and Music: Marilyn Haskel © 2006 by Marilyn Haskel. Used by permission.

Marilyn Haskel

This song may be sung as a response to the reading.

FORM: Echo over eight-bar ostinato

LEVEL: Medium

LEARN TOGETHER:
- Teach echo phrase by phrase, out of meter.
- Sing the melody with the overlap.
- Teach bass part phrase by phrase.
- Sing the whole bass part.

SING TOGETHER:
- Begin the bass part and cantor melody together.
- Cue the echo to begin on the down beat.

Words and Music: Marilyn Haskel, © 2006 by Marilyn Haskel. Used by permission.

35   I am thirsty

Marilyn Haskel

FORM: Call and response

LEVEL: Medium

LEARN AND SING TOGETHER:
- Say, "When I say 'I am thirsty,' your response is, 'I come to Jesus.'"
- Continue to teach the words this way, phrase by phrase.
- Teach the music for the congregational responses.
- Direct the congregation to respond to your call. Harmony may be improvised.
- If desired, a second cantor may join the first, singing the harmony part.

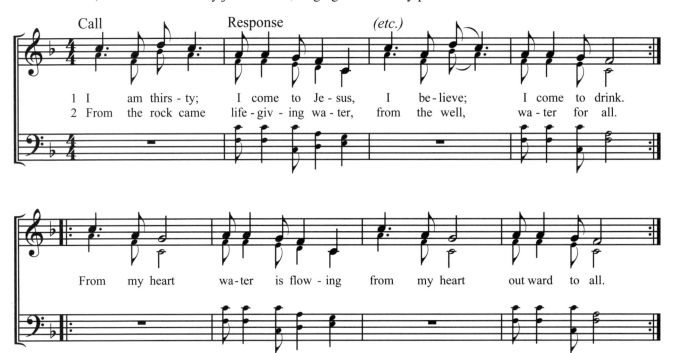

1 I am thirs-ty; I come to Je-sus, I be-lieve; I come to drink.
2 From the rock came life-giv-ing wa-ter, from the well, wa-ter for all.

From my heart wa-ter is flow-ing from my heart out-ward to all.

Words and Music: Marilyn Haskel, based on John 7:37-39, © 2006 by Marilyn Haskel. Used by permission.

Marilyn Haskel

This song is appropriate for baptisms or funerals.

FORM: Call and response

LEVEL: Medium

LEARN TOGETHER:
- Sing both the call and response of the first half of the piece to familiarize the congregation.
- Teach the responses, "in that Heaven" and "I know I gotta home at last."
- Sing the second half of the piece as you did the first to familiarize the congregation.
- Teach the response, "and tell the news."

SING TOGETHER:
- Begin the piece, cueing and singing the responses.
- Harmonies will be intuited by the congregation, or supported by a choir.

Music continues on next page.

An - gel,   Go, Sis - ter,   Go,

and tell the news.   and tell the news.

El - der,   I know I got a home at last.

and tell the news: I know I got a home at last.

Words: "Penny Jessye's Deathbed Spiritual", trans. by Eva A. Jessye, © 1994 by Jane Hirshfield in
    Women in Praise of the Sacred, Harper Collins Publishers.
Music: Marilyn Haskel, © 2007 by Marilyn Haskel. Used by permission.

Marilyn Haskel

This is a lively gospel acclamation or hymn of praise.

FORM: Layered

LEVEL: Easy

LEARN AND SING TOGETHER:
- Divide the congregation into four groups.
- Teach Part 1.

- Teach Part 2.

- Teach Part 3.

37   Gloria, hallelujah

• Teach Part 4 (descant).

Ho - san - na   Ho - san - na   Ho - san - na   Ho - san - na

Ho - san - na   Ho - san - na   hal - le - lu - jah.

• Sing all four parts together

Descant - Part 4

Ho san na   Ho san na   Ho san na   Ho san na

Part 1

Glo ri - a, _____   hal le - lu - jah. _____   Glo - ri - a, _____   hal - le - lu - jah. _____

Part 2

Glo ri - a, _____   hal le - lu - jah. _____   Glo - ri - a, _____   hal - le - lu - jah. _____

Part 3

Glo ri - a _____   Glo - ri - a _____   Glo - ri - a _____   Glo - ri - a _____

Music: Marilyn Haskel, © 2006 by Marilyn Haskel. Used by permission.

• If desired, teach the clapping part before or after you teach the singing parts.
• Ask the congregation to say (in rhythm): "Glo-ri-a, ho-san-na!" and then clap what they've spoken.

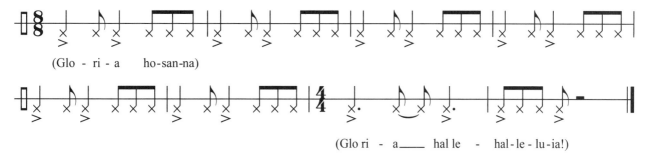

• Sing all parts with clapping.

38 Kyrie eleison/Mercer Kyrie eleison

Marilyn Haskel

When using this song in worship, a bell or finger cymbals may be used to signal when to move to the words "Christe eleison" and then back to "Kyrie eleison."

FORM: Layered

LEVEL: Easy

LEARN TOGETHER:
- Divide the congregation into three groups.
- Teach Part 1.

Ky - ri - e   e - le - i - son._____
Chri - ste   e - le - i - son._____
Ky - ri - e   e - le - i - son._____

- Teach Part 2.

Ky - ri - e   e - le - i - son._____
Chri - ste   e - le - i - son._____
Ky - ri - e   e - le - i - son._____

- Teach Part 3.

Ky - ri - e e - le - i - son._____
Chri - ste e - le - i - son._____
Ky - ri - e e - le - i - son._____

SING TOGETHER:

• Bring in each group one by one.

Part 1

Ky - ri - e   e - le - i - son._____
Chri - ste   e - le - i - son._____
Ky - ri - e   e - le - i - son._____

Part 2

Ky - ri - e   e - le - i - son._____
Chri - ste   e - le - i - son._____
Ky - ri - e   e - le - i - son._____

Part 3

Ky - ri - e   e - le - i - son._____
Chri - ste   e - le - i - son._____
Ky - ri - e   e - le - i - son._____

Setting: Marilyn Haskel, © 2006 by Marilyn Haskel. Used by permission.

39   Kyrie eleison/Kyrie on Five Notes

Marilyn Haskel

FORM: Layered

LEVEL: Easy

LEARN TOGETHER:
- Divide the congregation into four parts.
- Teach Part 1.

- Teach Part 2.

- Teach Part 3.

- Teach Part 4.

SING TOGETHER:
- Bring in each group one by one.
- Note the pick up in part one.
- Allow each part to become established before bringing in the next.

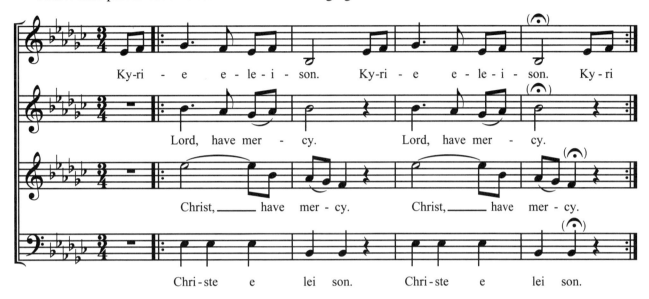

Setting: Marilyn Haskel, ©2006 by Marilyn Haskel. Used by permission.

40   Holy, holy, holy Lord/Mercer Sanctus

Marilyn Haskel

FORM: Simple Melody

LEVEL: Easy

LEARN AND SING TOGETHER:
- Teach in two bar phases.
- Sing the whole piece.
- Soon the congregation will have this piece memorized.

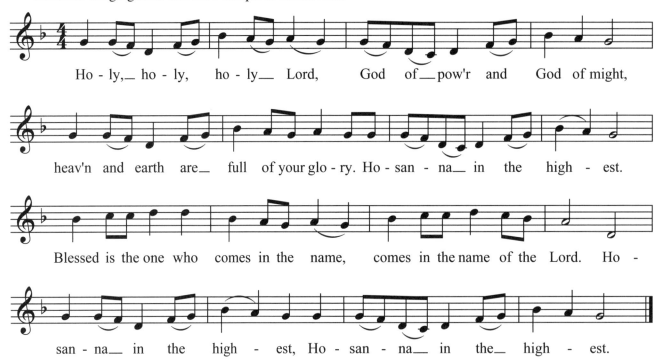

Music: based on the tune *Jefferson* from *Southern Harmony*, 1835, Marilyn Haskel, © 2006 by Marilyn Haskel.
Used by permission.

We praise you, we bless you/Mercer Memorial Acclamation   41

Marilyn Haskel

FORM: Layered

LEARN AND SING TOGETHER:
• Teach Part 1.

We praise you, we bless you, we give thanks.

• Teach Part 2.

We give thanks to you, and we pray to you, Lord our God.

• Combine parts have low voices sing their part through once before adding the high voices.
• In the eucharist this should be sung no more than two times by all.

High voices

We give thanks   to you,   and we pray to you,   Lord our God.

Low voices

We praise   you,   we bless   you,   we give   thanks.

Music: Marilyn Haskel, © 2007 by Marilyn Haskel. Used by permission.

42   Holy, holy, holy Lord/Sanctus on Six Notes

Marilyn Haskel

FORM: Simple Melody

LEVEL: Easy

LEARN AND SING TOGETHER:
- Teach "Hosanna in the highest."
- Sing the piece through yourself bringing in the congregation on "Hosanna in the highest."
- With a repetition or two, they will be able to join you for the rest of the piece.
- Alternatively you could then teach the first two measures echo style, then the 2nd two, and finally the entire "Blest is the one" phrase.

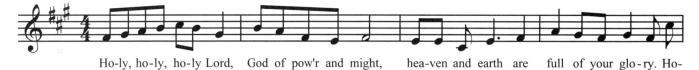

Ho-ly, ho-ly, ho-ly Lord, God of pow'r and might, hea-ven and earth are full of your glo-ry. Ho-

san-na in the high - est. Ho - san na in the high - est. Blest is the one who comes in the name of the

Lord._____ Ho - san - na in the high - est. Ho - san - na in the high - est.

Music: Marilyn Haskel, © 2006 by Marilyn Haskel. Used by permission.

Marilyn Haskel

FORM: Round

LEVEL: Easy

LEARN AND SING TOGETHER:
- Teach the round phrase by phrase.
- Divide the congregation into three groups.
- Bring the groups in one by one.

- In the eucharist this should be sung once through by each part.

Dy-ing, you des-troyed our death. Ri-sing, you re-stored our life. Christ Je-sus, come in glo-ry!

Words: *Enriching Our Worship 1,* © 1998 Church Publishing [www.churchpublishing.org]. Used by permission.
Music: Marilyn Haskel, © 2007 by Marilyn Haskel. Used by permission.

44 Our Father in heaven

Marilyn Haskel

FORM: Echo with harmonies sung by cantors

LEVEL: Medium

LEARN AND SING TOGETHER:
- Sing the piece, bringing in the congregation on the echo of each phrase.

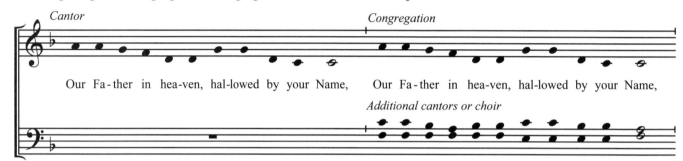

- Have two or more cantors or the choir join the congregation with harmony on the echo.

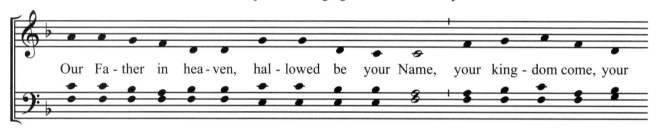

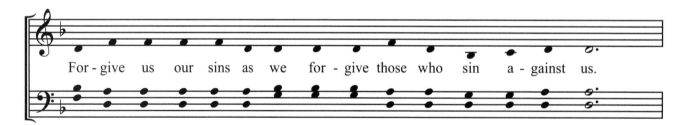

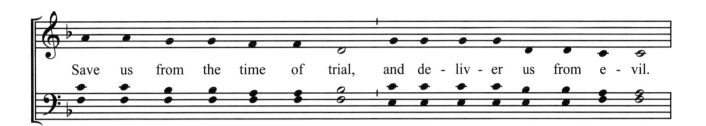

Save us from the time of trial, and de - liv - er us from e - vil.

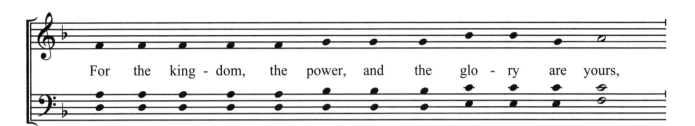

For the king - dom, the power, and the glo - ry are yours,

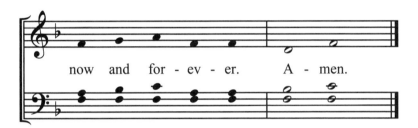

now and for - ev - er.   A - men.

Words: Book of Common Prayer
Music: Marilyn Haskel, © 2007 by Marilyn Haskel. Used by permission.

45   The bread which we break

Marilyn Haskel

FORM: Call and response

LEVEL: Easy

LEARN TOGETHER:
  • Teach Response 1

Hal-le - lu, hal-le-lu - jah.

  • Teach Response 2

Hal-le - lu, hal-le-lu - jah.

Sing Together:
- Sing the piece, bringing the congregation in on the responses.
- When you reach the final bar, indicate that this is the final phrase. Use your hands to imply the change in the response—the congregation will intuit the notes to sing.

Music continues on next page.

Marilyn Haskel

FORM: Simple melody over ostinato

LEVEL: Easy

LEARN TOGETHER:
   • Teach the ostinato to the low voices.

Bread of the world, this is   bread of the world

   • Teach the melody to the high voice, phrase by phrase.

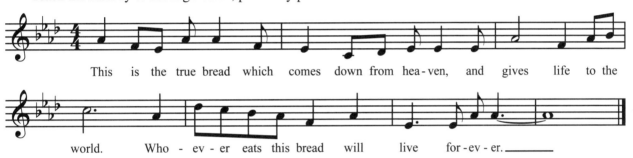

This   is   the true bread   which   comes   down from hea - ven,   and   gives   life   to the

world.   Who - ev - er   eats this bread   will   live   for - ev - er._____

Setting: Marilyn Haskel, © 2007 by Marilyn Haskel. Used by permission

46   **This is the true bread**

Sɪɴɢ Tᴏɢᴇᴛʜᴇʀ:
- Begin the ostinato.
- Bring in the high voices on the melody.

Words: *Enriching Our Worship 1,* © 1998 by Church Publishing [www.churchpublishing.org]. Used by permission.
Music: Marilyn Haskel, © 2007 by Marilyn Haskel. Used by permission.

Emily Scott

FORM: Echo

LEVEL: Easy

LEARN AND SING TOGETHER:
- Sing each phrase and bring in each echo.
- Give rhythmic clarity around each entrance, as the phrase length is irregular.

Music continues on next page.

Words: Greek, 3rd c., tr. F. Bland Tucker (1895-1984), adapt. by Emily Scott. Used by permission.
Music: Emily Scott, © 2007 by Emily Scott. Used by permission.

FORM: Layered with cantor part

LEVEL: Easy

LEARN AND SING TOGETHER:
- Divide the congregation into three groups.
- Teach Part 1.

- Teach Part 2.

- Teach Part 3.

• Bring in the parts one by one.
• Cue Part 3 on entrances until they are established.
• Bring in the cantor part.

and   blessed are   you   her on - ly   Son.
who   dwells in   the   e - ter - nal   light.
and   in   the high - est heav'n a - dored.

Come light   the lamps.   Come light   the lamps.

Come light   the lamps.   Come light   the lamps.

lamps.   Come light the

Words: Greek, 3rd c., tr. F. Bland Tucker, adapt. by Emily Scott. Used by permission.
Music: Emily Scott, © 2007 by Emily Scott. Used by permission.

49 Alleluia!

Holly Phares

FORM: Refrain

LEVEL: Easy

LEARN AND SING TOGETHER:
- Teach the refrain phrase by phrase.

Al - le - lu - ia! Al - le lu - ia! Al - le - lu - ia, a - men!

Al le lu - ia! Al - le - lu - ia! Al - le - lu - ia, a - men!

- Begin the verses, bringing in the refrain after each verse.
- When the pattern is established, bring in a cantor on the descant.

- If desired, accompany with drums.

Cantor Verse 1

He is a-live! He is a - live! The stone is rolled a - way! Em -

man - u - el, Christ Je - sus gives hope to us this day! Al-le- *Refrain*

Cantor Verse 2

He is a - live! He is a - live! Al - le - lu - ia, he is a - live!

Praise him! Praise him! Life your voi ces. Christ the Lord is a - live! Al le- *Refrain*

Cantor Verse 3

Day of glad - ness and re - joic - ing! Days of dark - ness are done! The

Lord of Love is here to stay! Al - le - lu - ia! Al - le

to final Refrain

Descant

Al - le - lu - ia! Al - le - lu - ia!

Refrain

lu - ia! Al - le lu - ia! Al - le - lu - ia, a - men! Al - le

Al - le - lu - ia! Al - le - lu - ia!

lu - ia! Al - le - lu - ia! Al - le - lu - ia, a - men!

50   Hosanna

Holly Phares

This piece may be sung with other texts, such as "Kyrie" or "Alleluia."

FORM: Layered

LEVEL: Easy
  • Divide the congregation into three groups.

LEARN TOGETHER:
  • Teach Part 1. (harmony optional)

Ho - san - na,   ho - san - na,   ho - san - na.

  • Teach Part 2.

Ho - san - na,   ho - san - na,   ho - san - na.

  • Teach Part 3.

Ho - - - san - na,   ho - san - - na.

92

SING TOGETHER:

- Bring in each group, one by one.

- If desired, an additional part may be added

Setting: Holly Phares, © 2004 by Holly Phares. Used by permission.

51 Hear my cry, O Lord

Holly Phares

FORM: Layered

LEVEL: Easy

LEARN TOGETHER:
- Divide the congregation into two groups.
- Teach Part 1.

- Teach Part 2.

SING TOGETHER
- Bring in the groups one by one.

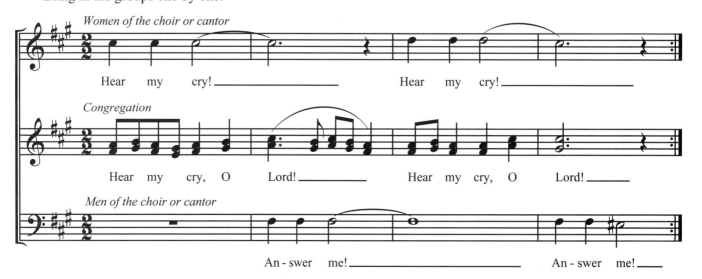

Music: Holly Phares, © 2001 by Holly Phares. Used by permission.

- If desired the choir parts may be sung by two other congregational groups.

Holly Phares

FORM: Simple melody

LEVEL: Easy

LEARN AND SING TOGETHER:
- Teach the melody phrase by phrase.
- Sing the whole melody.
- Begin to improvise harmony – the congregation will join you in improvising.

I am Spi - rit's Be - lov - ed_____ with whom God is well pleased.

I am Spi - rit's Be - lov - ed_____ with whom God is well pleased.

Words: Patricia Pearce, © 2005 by Patricia Pearce. Used by permission.
Music: Holly Phares, © 2005 by Holly Phares. Used by permission.

53   Hosanna/Hosanna in Canon

Holly Phares

FORM: Layered

LEVEL: Easy

LEARN TOGETHER:
- Divide the congregation into three groups.
- Teach Part 1. phrase by phrase.

Ho - san-na, ho - san-na, ho - san - na! Ho - san-na, ho - san-na, ho - san - na. Ho

- Teach Part 2 phrase by phrase.

Ho - san - na, ho-san - na, ho - san - na! Ho - san - na, ho-san - na, ho - san - na! Ho

- Teach Part 3 phrase by phrase.

Ho - san - na, ho - san - na! Ho - san - na, ho - san - na!

SING TOGETHER:
  • Bring in each group one by one.
  • Add a tambourine or a klezmer clarinet!

Setting: Holly Phares, © 2003 by Holly Phares. Used by permission.

54   Christ is our mirror

Mark Howe

FORM: Layered

LEVEL: Easy

LEARN TOGETHER:
- Divide the congregation into four groups.
- Teach Part 1.

- Teach Part 2.

- Teach Part 3.

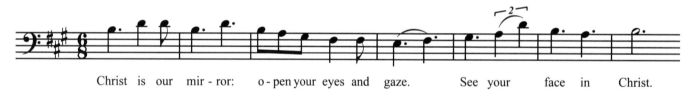

- Teach Part 4.

S<small>ING</small> T<small>OGETHER</small>:
   • Bring in each group one by one

Words: Odes of Solomon, paraphrased by Donald Schell.
Music: Mark Howe, © 2006 by Mark Howe. Used by permission.

55 The earth is the Lord's/Procession to the Table

Mark Howe

FORM: One two-bar and one eight-bar ostinato with a three-part melody for cantors

LEVEL: Easy

LEARN AND SING TOGETHER:
- • Divide the congregation into two groups.
- • Teach ostinato 1

The earth is the Lord's and all that is in it, the

world, the world, and all who dwell there - in.

- • Teach ostinato 2

The earth is the Lord's, the earth is the Lord's.

• Put the two parts together and keep the pattern going.
• When the singing is established, bring in the three cantors.
• If desired the djembe ostinato may be added.

Music continues on next page.

Lord and a   just re-ward   from the   God of their sal - va - - - tion.

earth   is the   Lord's   and   all   that is   in   it,   the   world,   the   world,   and

earth   is the   Lord's,   the   earth   is the   Lord's.   The   earth   is the   Lord's,   the

all   who   dwell   there - in.

earth   is   the   Lord's.   The   earth   is   the   Lord's.

Words: Psalm 24:1-6
Music: Mark Howe, © 2006 by Mark Howe. Used by permission.

56   To the bath and the table

Mark Howe

FORM: Round over cantor verses

LEVEL: Easy

LEARN TOGETHER:
- Teach the melody of the round phrase by phrase.
- Sing the whole melody.

Words: adapt. from *Holy Things* by Gordon W. Lathrop, © 1993 Fortress Press. Used by permission of Augsburg Fortress Publishers.
Music: Mark Howe, © 2007 by Mark Howe. Used by permission.

- Divide the congregation into three groups
- When the melody is established, sing as a round.

Sing Together:
- Bring in each group in the round one by one.
- Add the cantor singing the verses with the round.

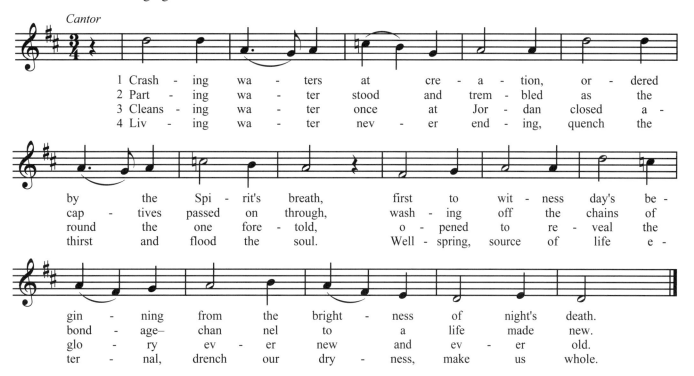

1 Crash - ing wa - ters at cre - a - tion, or - dered
2 Part - ing wa - ter stood and trem - bled as the
3 Cleans - ing wa - ter once at Jor - dan closed a -
4 Liv - ing wa - ter nev - er end - ing, quench the

by the Spi - rit's breath, first to wit - ness day's be -
cap - tives passed on through, wash - ing off the chains of
round the one fore - told, o - pened to re - veal the
thirst and flood the soul. Well - spring, source of life e -

gin - ning from the bright - ness of night's death.
bond - age— chan - nel to a life made new.
glo - ry ev - er new and ev - er old.
ter - nal, drench our dry - ness, make us whole.

Words: Sylvia G. Dunstan, © 1991 by GIA Publications, 7404 S. Mason Avenue, Chicago, IL 60638 [www.giamusic.com].
    Used by permission.
Music: Mark Howe, © 2007 by Mark Howe. Used by permission.

57   Come all, draw near and eat

Mark Howe

FORM: Refrain

LEVEL: Easy

LEARN AND SING TOGETHER:
  • Teach the congregational refrain.

Andante

Come all, _____ draw near and   eat. _____

  • Start the instrumental drone.

• Cantor sings the verses followed by the congregational refrain.

Your heavens are too high for us to reach. Come all, draw near and eat.

But here in your house you come close.

Your throne is a fire none can touch.

But here you live and dwell in bread and wine.

You come to us so we can touch you.

You draw us to you with cords of love.

You dwell ten-der-ly with us.

Words: Syrian, ca. 460, para. Donald Schell. Used by permission.
Music: Mark Howe, © 2006 by Mark Howe. Used by permission.

58   God bless every step

Ruth Cunningham

This Gaelic text comes from the Céile Dé, a Celtic Christian order.

FORM: Two-part ostinato with round

LEVEL: Easy

LEARN TOGETHER:
   • Divide the congregation into three groups with one larger group to sing the round.
   • Teach Ostinato 1.

   • Teach Ostinato 2.

   • Teach the Round (note that the round begins in the middle of the second measure, not at the bar line.

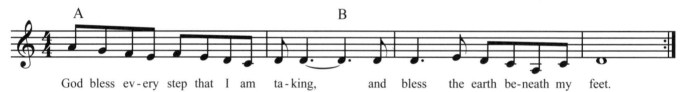

SING TOGETHER:
- Bring in each group one by one.

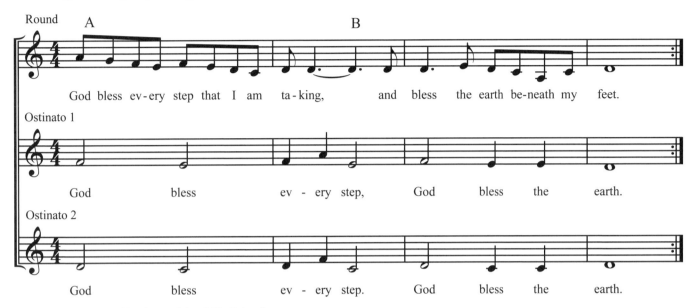

Words: tr. from a Celtic chant of the Céile Dé order.
Music: Ruth Cunningham, © 2007 by Ruth Cunningham. Used by permission.

59 Come light of lights

Ruth Cunningham

FORM: Double five-part round

LEVEL: Easy

LEARN TOGETHER:
- Divide the congregation into two groups.
- Teach Part 1 phrase by phrase.

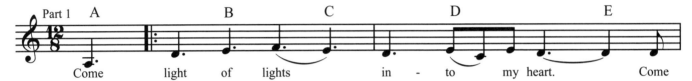

- Teach Part 2 phrase by phrase.

SING TOGETHER:
- Bring in both parts one by one.
- When the melodies are well established try singing as a round as indicated.

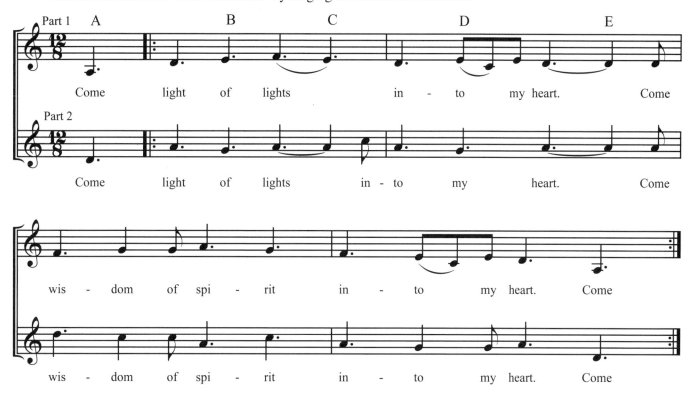

Words: tr. from a Celtic chant of the Céile Dé order.
Music: Ruth Cunningham, © 2006 by Ruth Cunningham. Used by permission.

- May be sung with as few as two round groups on each part.

60   Open my heart to your light

Ruth Cunningham

FORM: Layered

LEVEL: Easy

LEARN TOGETHER:
- Divide the congregation into four groups.
- Teach Part 1.

- Teach Part 2.

- Teach Part 3.

- Teach Part 4.

SING TOGETHER:
- Bring in each group one by one.

O-pen my heart to your light and truth, O-pen my heart.

O-pen my heart to your light, O-pen my heart to your truth.

O - - - pen my heart.

O - - - pen my heart.

Words and music: Ruth Cunningham, © 2007 by Ruth Cunningham. Used by permission.

61   Arise, shine

Ruth Cunningham

This song is particularly appropriate Christmas and Epiphany

Form: Layered

Level: Easy

Learn Together:
- Divide the congregation into two groups.
- Teach Part 1 to the first group.

A - rise,   shine,   for your light   has   come,   and the

glo - ry   of the Lord   has   dawned   up - on   you.   A

- Teach Part 2 to the second group.

A - rise,   shine   for your   light   has   come,   and the

glo - ry   of the Lord   has   dawned   up - on   you.   A

Sɪɴɢ Tᴏɢᴇᴛʜᴇʀ:
- Bring in each group one by one.

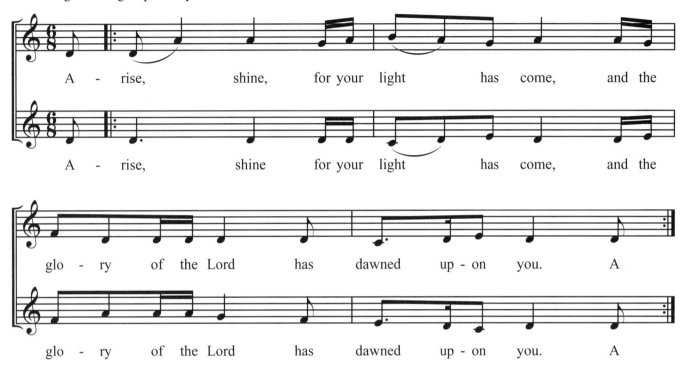

A - rise,   shine,   for your   light   has   come,   and the

A - rise,   shine   for your   light   has   come,   and the

glo - ry   of the Lord   has   dawned   up - on   you.   A

glo - ry   of the Lord   has   dawned   up - on   you.   A

Words: Isaiah 60:1
Music: Ruth Cunningham, © 2007 by Ruth Cunningham. Used by permission.

62   God, your people seek shelter

Ruth Cunningham

FORM: One-bar ostinato and four-bar refrain for congregation with cantor.

LEVEL: Medium

LEARN TOGETHER:
- Divide the congregation into two groups.
- Teach the ostinato to the first group.

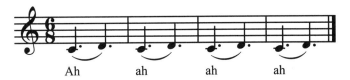

- Teach refrain to the second group.

SING TOGETHER:
- Begin the ostinato.
- Bring in the refrain, then direct them to join in on the ostinato for four bars.
- Bring the cantor.

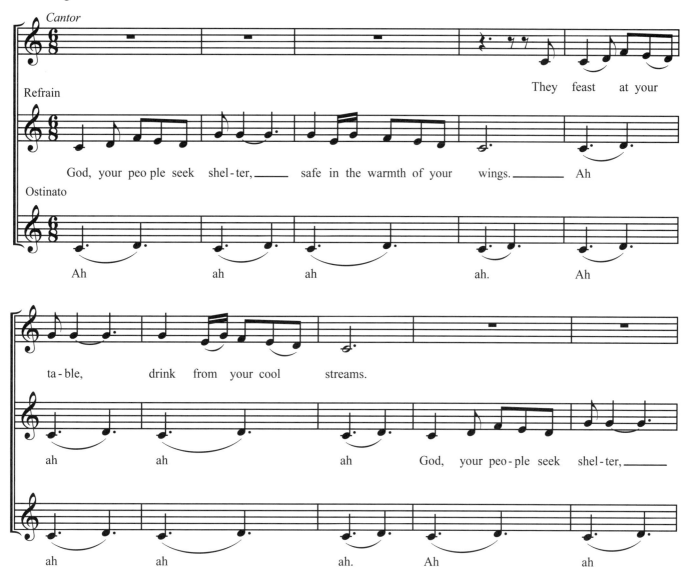

Music continues on next page.

You are the fount of life, you give us light and we see.

safe in the warmth of your wings.___ Ah   ah   ah   ah

ah   ah.   Ah   ah   ah   ah.

God,   your peo - ple seek shel - ter,___ safe   in the warmth of your   wings.___

Ah   ah   ah   ah.

Words: based on Psalm 36:7.
Music: Ruth Cunningham, © 2007 by Ruth Cunningham. Used by permission.

Ruth Cunningham

This Gaelic text means: Come, Lord, come thou Being. This beautiful text comes from the Céile Dé, a Celtic Christian order.

FORM: Simple Melody

LEVEL: Easy

LEARN AND SING TOGETHER:
- Teach the words which are pronounced: tahr ah hear-nah, tahr-ah-hee.
- Teach the melody phrase by phrase.
- Try the whole melody with words.
- Begin improvising harmonies – your congregation will follow your lead.

Words: Fonn or Celtic chant from the order of Céile Dé.
Music: Ruth Cunningham, © 2006 by Ruth Cunningham. Used by permission.

64   We are walking

Ed Thompson

FORM: Layered with optional two-part cantor line

LEVEL: Easy

LEARN TOGETHER:
- Divide the congregation into three groups.
- Teach Part 1 to the first group phrase by phrase.

Refrain Part 1

Walk - ing,   oh we are walk - ing,   oh we are walk - ing, walk - ing,   oh. _____

Walk - ing,   oh we are walk - ing,   oh we are walk - - - ing.

- Teach Part 2 (melody) to the second group phrase by phrase.

We are walk-ing,   we are walk - ing   with the light   of   Christ.

We are walk - ing,   we are walk-ing   in the love   of   God.

- Teach Part 3 to the third group phrase by phrase.

We are walk - ing,   we are walk - ing   with the light   of   Christ;

we are walk - ing,   we are walk - ing   in the love   of   God.

S<small>ING</small> T<small>OGETHER</small>:
- Bring each group in one by one.

Refrain ♩ = 112

Part 3

We are walk-ing, we are walk-ing with the light of Christ;

Part 2 (melody)

We are walk-ing, we are walk-ing with the light of Christ.

Part 1

Walk-ing, oh we are walk-ing, oh we are walk - ing, walk - ing, oh. _____

we are walk-ing, we are walk-ing in the love of God.

We are walk - ing, we are walk-ing in the love of God.

Walk - ing, oh we are walk - ing, oh we are walk - - - - ing.

Words and music: Ed Thompson, © 2007 by Ed Thompson. Used by permission.

• If desired, bring in the two cantors to sing the verses alternating with the refrain.

Peace   the goal   and   peace   the way,   no mat-ter where   the   road may lead;
Patience the goal   and   patience the way,   no mat-ter where   the   road may lead;

peace   the goal   and   peace   the way,   this we will hold   in   thought and deed.
patience the goal   and   patience the way,   this we will hold   in   thought and deed.

Words and music: Ed Thompson, © 2007 by Ed Thompson. Used by permission.

• If desired, add these percussion parts.

Ben Allaway

This song uses the South African method of singing instructions in the body of the song. Once the two responses are learned, the cantor cues the congregation to switch between them by singing their words first. From this point on no verbal instructions are needed.

FORM: Call and response

LEVEL: Medium

LEARN TOGETHER:
- Teach the first response by the echo method and repeat until secure.

- Teach the second response as you did the first.

65   Freedom come

SING TOGETHER:

• Sing the call and bring in each response as indicated. The rest of the piece teaches itself.

Music continues on next page.

65 Freedom come

Words and music: Ben Allaway, © 2006 by Ben Allaway. Used by permission.

Ben Allaway

This piece uses only two echoed phrases and is a satisfying end to worship. It uses the South African method of singing instructions within the song. Once the two phrases are learned, the cantor cues the congregation to switch between them by singing their words first. From this point on no verbal instructions are needed.

FORM: Echo

LEVEL: Medium

LEARN AND SING TOGETHER:
• Teach the first echoed phrase.

• Teach the second echoed phrase.

• The rest of the piece teaches itself – just follow the score!
Note the rhythmic change for the phrase "The way of peace. . ." The congregation will need direction at this point.

Music continues on next page.

66   From this house

Words and music: Ben Allaway © 2007 by Ben Allaway. Used by permission.

67   Hosanna, ho!/Palm Sunday Processional

Ben Allaway

FORM: Echo

LEVEL: Easy

LEARN AND SING TOGETHER:
- Sing each phrase, directing the congregation to repeat after you.

Words: Mt 21:9
Music: Ben Allaway, © 2007 by Ben Allaway. Used by permission.

FORM: Overlapping echo with choir

LEVEL: Medium

LEARN TOGETHER:
- Divide the congregation into low and high voices.
- Teach the melody to everyone phrase by phrase.

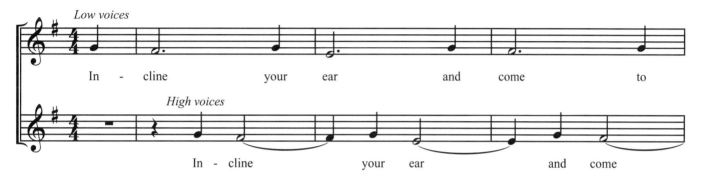

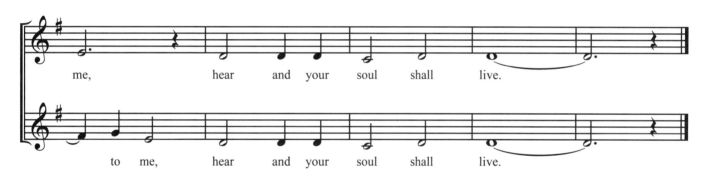

- Begin the choir part on the "Oh."

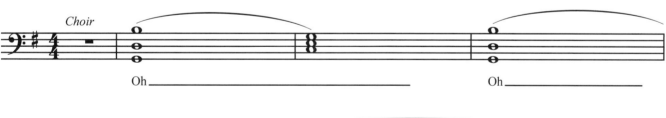

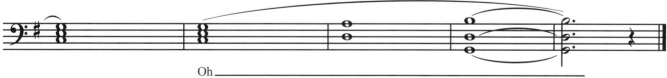

SING TOGETHER:

• After the choir is established, lead the melody, giving cues to bring the congregation in on the overlapping echo.

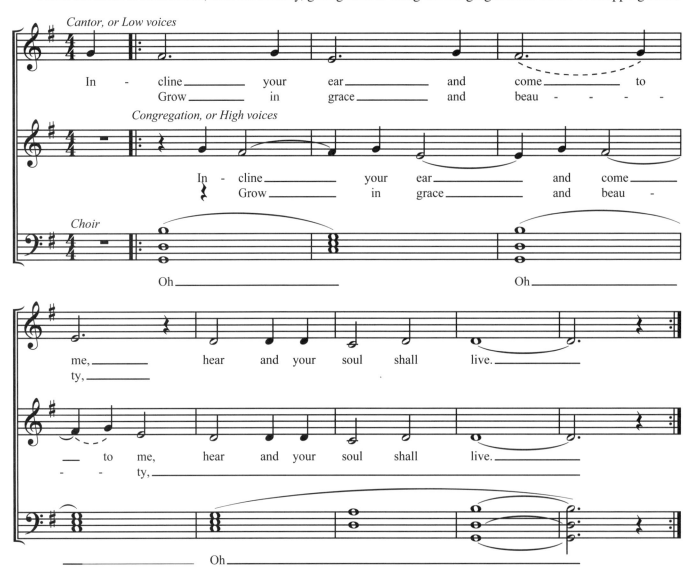

Words: Isaiah 1:3, paraphrased in "God Calling" ed. by A.E. Russell. Used by permission.
Music: Ben Allaway, © 2007 by Ben Allaway. Used by permission.

Ben Allaway

FORM: Echo

LEVEL: Easy

LEARN AND SING TOGETHER:
- Sing each phrase, directing the congregation to repeat after you.
- Add a Celtic drum or djembe if desired.

Bright and exuberant

Music continues on next page.

Music: Ben Allaway, © 2006 by Ben Allaway. Used by permission.

70   I am giving thee worship/Celtic Offering

Ben Allaway

This call and response piece depends on the cantor to call out words for the upcoming phrase. Instead of explaining how the piece works, simply use strong and obvious direction to show the congregation when to sing and when to listen.

FORM: Call and response

LEVEL: Medium

LEARN AND SING TOGETHER:

    • Begin by singing the following phrase alone to understand the melodic flow.

- As you do this, point to yourself for the words you will sing alone and point to the congregation for the words they will sing with you.
- Then try the whole verse with everyone, again indicating with gestures when they should listen or sing.
- Go on to the second verse with new words. Soon they'll have the pattern down.

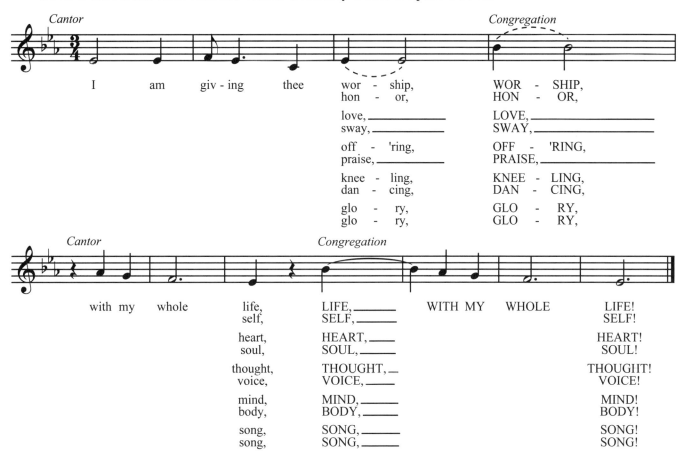

Words: Esther De Waal from *The Celtic Way of Prayer,* © 1997 by Esther De Waal, adapt. by Ben Allaway.
Music: Ben Allaway, © 2006 by Ben Allaway. Used by permission.

71 I will supply your need

Ben Allaway

FORM: Call and response

LEVEL: Easy

LEARN AND SING TOGETHER:
  • Teach the response.

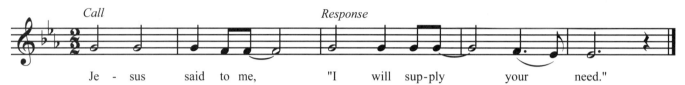

  • Sing the piece phrase by phrase, bringing in the congregation on the response.

140

The right-eous need my pi-ty for sin-ners.

The lone-ly need my friend ship.

The fight-ers need my lead ing.

No one of this world can be all these to an oth - er.

Sing it o - ver.

Be - lieve him when he says,

Hal - le - lu - jah!

Thank you Lord!

72   My soul is a river

Ben Allaway

FORM: Simple melody

LEVEL: Easy

LEARN AND SING TOGETHER:
- Sing the first verse once through.
- Repeat and indicate that the congregation should join you.
- When you reach the second verse, indicate that the congregation should listen until the repeat.
  Soon they will pick up on the words.
- All should sing the third verse, following the cues in the score to feed the congregation the last two bars.

Words: Amos 5:24 and Ben Allaway, © 2004 by Santa Barbara Music Publishing. Used by permission.
Music: Ben Allaway, © 2004 by Santa Barbara Music Publishing. Used by permission.

73 Justice is moving

Ben Allaway

FORM: Echo

LEVEL: Easy

LEARN AND SING TOGETHER:
   • Sing the piece phrase by phrase, directing the congregation to repeat after you.

Words and music: Ben Allaway, © 2006 by Ben Allaway. Used by permission.

74   Get up, children!

Ben Allaway

Instead of giving verbal instructions, sing this song when inviting children to come forward.

FORM: Echo

LEVEL: Easy

LEARN AND SING TOGETHER:
- Sing the piece phrase by phrase, directing the congregation to repeat after you.

Words and music: Ben Allaway, © 2004 by Thresholds Music Press, DesMoines, IA, 515-288-8883. Used by permission.

75   Goodness of sea be thine

Judith Dodge

FORM: Layered

LEVEL: Easy

LEARN TOGETHER:
- Divide the congregation into four groups.
- Teach Part 1.

- Teach Part 2.

- Teach Part 3.

- Teach Part 4.

- Teach Part 5.

SING TOGETHER:
- Bring the groups in one by one.

Goodness of sea be thine. Goodness of earth be thine, goodness of heaven.

Words: from *Carmina Gadelica: Hymns and Incantations Collected in the Highlands and Islands of Scotland in the Last Century* by Alexander Carmichael.
Music: Judith Dodge, © 2006 by Judith Dodge. Used by permission.

76   Sing praise to God/Song of Praise

Judith Dodge

FORM: Round

LEVEL: Easy

LEARN AND SING TOGETHER:
  • Teach the melody phrase by phrase.
  • Divide the congregation into two groups.
  • Bring in the second group when group one reaches letter B.

Judith Dodge

FORM: Simple melody

LEVEL: Easy

LEARN AND SING TOGETHER:
- Teach the melody phrase by phrase.
- Teach the clapping pattern and repeat until it is established.
- Sing the melody with the clapping.

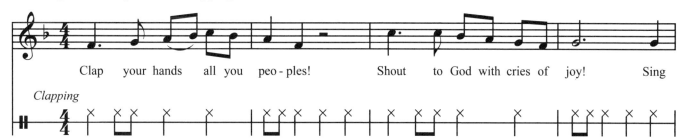

Clap your hands all you peo - ples! Shout to God with cries of joy! Sing

Clapping

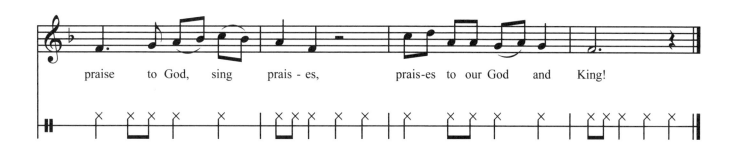

praise to God, sing prais - es, prais-es to our God and King!

Words: Psalm 47:1, 6
Music: Judith Dodge, © 2006 by Judith Dodge. Used by permission.

78 Any who wish/The Great Entrance

Judith Dodge

This music may be sung as the elements are brought forward and the table set for eucharist.

FORM: Congregational refrain

LEVEL: Easy

LEARN AND SING TOGETHER:
- Teach the congregational refrain.
- Begin a drone on G and D.
- Begin the cantor verses over the drone.
- Bring the congregation in on the refrain.

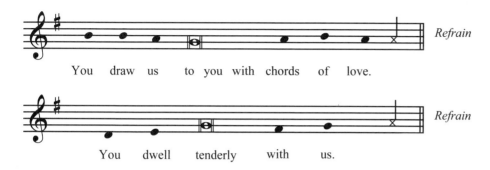

Refrain

You draw us to you with chords of love.

Refrain

You dwell tenderly with us.

Words: Syrian, ca. 460.
Music: Judith Dodge, © 2006 by Judith Dodge. Used by permission.

• If desired, finger cymbals may be added at the end of each phrase.

79   Out of Zion

Judith Dodge

FORM: Simple melody

LEVEL: Easy

LEARN AND SING TOGETHER:
- Teach the melody phrase by phrase.
- Sing the whole melody.
- When the melody is established, begin to improvise harmonies – the congregation will follow your lead.

Out of Zi - on per-fect in beau - ty, God ap-pears to us in glo - ry. us in glo - ry.

Words: Psalm 50:2
Music: Judith Dodge, © 2006 by Judith Dodge. Used by permission.

154

Bill Doggett

FORM: Round

LEVEL: Easy

LEARN AND SING TOGETHER:
- Teach the round phrase by phrase.
- Divide the congregation into three groups.
- Bring in the second group when group one reaches letter B and so on.

I will   sing a song of mer - cy;   sing   a   song of jus - tice;   sing   a   song of praise   to

God.   I will   live a life of mer-cy;   live a life of jus-tice,   live a life of praise to   God.

Words: paraphrase of Psalm 101 by William J. Doggett, © 2001 by William J. Doggett. Used by permission.
Music: William J. Doggett, © 2001 by William J. Doggett. Used by permission.

81   When I was in trouble/God Was There

Bill Doggett

FORM: Round

LEVEL: Easy

LEARN AND SING TOGETHER:
- Teach the round phrase by phrase.
- Divide the congregation into two groups.
- Bring in the second group when group one reaches letter B.

Round

When I was in trou ble, I called out to God.   I called out to God,   and God was   there.

William J. Doggett

This song is a great hit, especially with children. It may be sung as written or as a cumulative song where additional verses are added one at a time and repeated consecutively with each repetition.

Form: Simple melody

Level: Easy

Learn and Sing Together:
- Teach the refrain phrase by phrase.
- Sing the whole refrain.
- Lead the "clap your hands" section, then go back to the refrain.

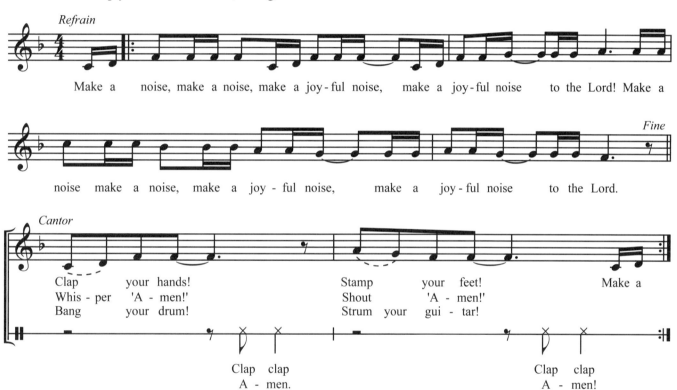

Refrain

Make a noise, make a noise, make a joy - ful noise, make a joy - ful noise to the Lord! Make a

noise make a noise, make a joy - ful noise, make a joy - ful noise to the Lord. *Fine*

Cantor

Clap your hands!   Stamp your feet!   Make a
Whis - per 'A - men!'   Shout 'A - men!'
Bang your drum!   Strum your gui - tar!

Clap clap   Clap clap
A - men.   A - men!

Words: paraphrase of Psalm 81 by William J. Doggett, © 2001 by William J. Doggett. Used by permission.
Music: William J. Doggett, © 2001 by William J. Doggett. Used by permission.

83 Holy, holy, holy Lord/Sanctus

Bill Blomquist

FORM: Echo

LEVEL: Easy

LEARN AND SING TOGETHER:
- Sing the piece phrase by phrase, directing the congregation to repeat after you.

Setting: Bill Blomquist. © 2007 by Blomquistian Music Ltd. Used by permission.

• If desired a hand drum may be played on the first beat of every measure.

84   Spirits rising

Lisa Levine

The refrain of this song is a Nigun or Hassidic melody often with no words which is sung to express and stir one's soul.

FORM: Echo

LEVEL: Easy

LEARN AND SING TOGETHER:
- Sing the piece phrase by phrase, directing the congregation to repeat after you.

Slow

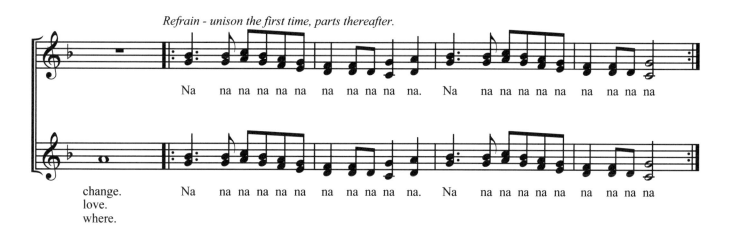

Refrain - unison the first time, parts thereafter.

Na na na na na na na na na na na. Na na na na na na na na na

change.
love.
where.

Na na na na na na na na na na na. Na na na na na na na na na

Words and music: Lisa Levine, © 2007 by Lisa Levine. Used by permission.

85 Our Father in heaven/Lord's Prayer

Sanford Dole

FORM: Echo

LEVEL: Easy

LEARN AND SING TOGETHER:
  • Sing the piece phrase by phrase, directing the congregation to repeat after you.

Words: Book of Common Prayer
Music: Sanford Dole, © 2001 All Saints Company. Used by permission.

Sources of Texts

Allaway, Ben	65, 66, 72, 73, 74	*Odes of Solomon*	54
Amos 5:24	72	Page, Nick	11
Antiphon for Psalm 134	26	Palo-Cherwien, Susan	10
Bickersteth, Edward H., Jr. (1875)	7	Pearce, Patricia	52
Book of Common Prayer	3, 4, 5, 6, 8, 38, 39,	Psalm 24:1-6	55
	41, 42, 44, 83, 85	Psalm 24:7-10	1
Book of Occasional Services	45	Psalm 34	26
Carmichael, Alexander	75	Psalm 36:7	62
Carmina Gadelica	75	Psalm 43:3	9
Celtic chant of the Ciéle Dé order	32, 58, 59, 63	Psalm 47:1,6	77
Chinese mantra	31	Psalm 50:14	17
Cunningham, Ruth	60	Psalm 50:2	79
De Waal, Esther	70	Psalm 81	82
Dodge, Judith	76	Psalm 101	80
Dunstan, Sylvia	56	Psalm 120:1	81
Enriching Our Worship 1	43, 46	Psalm 139:11	15
Everett, Isaac	23, 24	Psalm 141:2	16
Free Church of Scotland	9	Psalm 150:6	25
Genesis 1:27	18	Romans 8:14-27	19
Greek, 3rd c.	47, 48	Russell, A. E.	71
Haskel, Marilyn	33, 34	Schell, Donald	54
Hudson, Michael	14	Scott, Emily	47, 48
Isaiah 1:3	68	Schell, Donald	92, 96
Isaiah 60:1	61	Silesius, Angelus (1624-1677)	27, 28, 29, 30
Jessye, Eva A.	36	Snodgrass, j	23, 24
John 7: 37-39	35	*Southern Harmony, 1835*	40
Julian of Norwich, (ca. 1342-1413)	12, 13	Syrian, ca. 460	57, 78
Lathrop, Gordon	56	Traditional	3, 37, 49, 50
Law, Eric H. F.	21, 22	Thompson, Ed	64
Levine, Lisa	84	Tucker, F. Bland	47, 48
Matthew 5:44	20		
Matthew 21:9	67		

Indexes

Composers Index

Allaway, Ben	65, 66, 67, 68, 69, 70, 71, 72, 73, 74
Blomquist, Bill	83
Cunningham, Ruth	58, 59, 60, 61, 62, 63
Dodge, Judith	75, 76, 77, 78, 79
Doggett, Bill	80, 81, 82
Dole, Sanford	85
Everett, Isaac	23, 24
Frahm, Frederick	10
Gay, Sandra	14
Haskel, Marilyn	33, 34, 35, 36, 37, 38, 39, 40, 41, 42, 43
Hernández, Ana	25, 26, 27, 28, 29, 30, 31, 32
Howe, Mark	54, 55, 56, 57
Law, Eric H.F.	15, 16, 17, 18, 19, 20, 21, 22
Levine, Lisa	84
McClellan, Robinson	1, 2, 3,4, 5, 6, 7, 8, 9
Page, Nick	11
Phares, Holly	49, 50, 51, 52, 53
Roberts, William Bradley	12, 13
Scott, Emily	47, 48
Snodgrass, j	23, 24
Thompson, Ed	64

Topical Index

Popular titles are bold.

Acclamations

Alleluia - McClellan	2
Alleluia - Phares	49
Antiphon for Whirling	26
Celtic Offering	70
Christ has died	5
Clap your hands	77
Dying, you destroyed our death	43
Get up, children!	74
Gloria, hallelujah	37
Holy, holy, holy Lord - Blomquist	83
Holy, holy, holy Lord - Haskel	40
Holy, holy, holy Lord - Haskel	42
Holy, holy, holy Lord - Robinson	4
Hosanna	50
Hosanna	53
Hosanna in Canon	53
Hosanna, ho!	67
I am giving thee worship	70
I will sing a song of mercy	80
I'm walking with my God today	11
Kol hanneshama	25
Lift up your heads	1
Make a noise!	82
Memorial Acclamation - McClellan	5
Memorial Acclamation on Six Notes	43
Mercer Memorial Acclamation	41
Mercer Sanctus	40
Out of Zion	79
Palm Sunday Processional	67
Sanctus and Benedictus - Blomquist	83
Sanctus and Benedictus - Robinson	4
Sanctus on Six Notes	42
Sing praise to God	76
Song of Praise	76
We are walking	64
We praise you, we bless you	41
Who Is This King?	1
Yours is the day	26

Bread and Wine

Any who wish may approach	78
Come all draw near and eat	57
Procession to the Table	55
The bread which we break	45
The earth is the Lord's	55
The Great Entrance	78
This is the true bread	46

Contemplation

All shall be well	12
Child of Mary	22
Christ is our mirror	54
God is a pure no--thing	27
Goodness of sea be thine	75
If in your heart	29
If in your heart	30
Incline your ear	68
Jesu, Jesu, Jesu	22
Let my prayer be set forth	16
Peace, perfect peace	7
Spirits rising	84
Where I go in the world	32
You have grounded my soul	13

Departing in Peace

Dismissal	24
From this house	66
I asked Lord Jesus	24

Light

Arise, shine	61
As the dark awaits the dawn	10
Come light of lights	59
Come light the lamps	48

Indexes

Darkness is not dark	15
Evening Canticle	34
Evening lamps are lit - Haskel	34
Evening lamps are lit - Hernández	28
Firelight Praise	28
Now daylight fades	33
O gracious light - McClellan	3
O gracious light - Scott	47
O send your light forth	9
Open my heart to your light	60
Phos Hilaron - Robinson	3
Phos Hilaron - Scott	47
Phos Hilaron - Scott	48

Prayers

Agnus Dei	6
Confession	23
Freedom come	65
God, your people seek shelter	62
Good Lord, in that heaven	36
Goodness of sea be thine	75
Hear my cry, O Lord!	51
I am the Spirit's Beloved	52
I will supply your need	71
Kyrie eleison	38
Kyrie eleison	39
Kyrie on Five Notes	39
Lamb of God	6
Let the broken ones be healed	14
Lord, have mercy	23
Mercer Kyrie eleison	38
Open my heart	31
Our Father in heaven - Dole	85
Our Father in heaven - Haskel	44
Our Father in heaven - Robinson	8
Peace, perfect peace	7
Spirits rising	84
Tar a thighearna tar a thi	63
The Lord's Prayer - Dole	85

The Lord's Prayer - Robinson	8

Service Music

Agnus Dei	6
Any who wish may approach	78
Christ has died	5
Come all draw near and eat	57
Come light the lamps	48
Dying, you destroyed our death	43
Holy, holy, holy Lord - Blomquist	83
Holy, holy, holy Lord - Haskel	40
Holy, holy, holy Lord - Haskel	42
Holy, holy, holy Lord - Robinson	4
Kyrie eleison	38
Kyrie eleison	39
Kyrie on Five Notes	39
Lamb of God	6
Memorial Acclamation - McClellan	5
Memorial Acclamation on Six Notes	43
Mercer Kyrie eleison	38
Mercer Memorial Acclamation	41
Mercer Sanctus	40
O gracious light - McClellan	3
O gracious light - Scott	47
Our Father in heaven - Dole	85
Our Father in heaven - Haskel	44
Our Father in heaven - Robinson	8
Phos Hilaron - Robinson	3
Phos Hilaron - Scott	47
Phos Hilaron - Scott	48
Procession to the Table	55
Sanctus and Benedictus - Blomquist	83
Sanctus and Benedictus - Robinson	4
Sanctus on Six Notes	42
The bread which we break	45
The earth is the Lord's	55
The Great Entrance	78
The Lord's Prayer - Dole	85
The Lord's Prayer - Robinson	8

This is the true bread 46

We praise you, we bless you 41

Water

Come with me to the springs 69

Crashing waters at creation 56

I am thirsty 35

Let the broken ones be healed 14

My soul is a river 72

To the bath and the table 56

Word

Christ is our guiding light 21

God bless every step 58

God Was There 81

In God's image I was created 18

Justice is moving 73

Kol hanneshama 25

Lift up your heads 1

Love your enemies 20

Offer to God a sacrifice 17

The groaning of the Spirit 19

When I was in trouble 81

Who Is This King? 1

Indexes

First Lines and Titles

Popular titles are bold.

Agnus Dei	6
All shall be well	12
Alleluia - McClellan	2
Alleluia - Phares	49
Antiphon for Whirling	26
Any who wish may approach	78
Arise, shine	61
As the dark awaits the dawn	10
Celtic Offering	70
Child of Mary	22
Christ has died	5
Christ is our guiding light	21
Christ is our mirror	54
Clap your hands	77
Come all draw near and eat	57
Come light of lights	59
Come light the lamps	48
Come with me to the springs	69
Confession	23
Crashing waters at creation	56
Darkness is not dark	15
Dismissal	24
Dying, you destroyed our death	43
Evening Canticle	34
Evening lamps are lit - Haskel	34
Evening lamps are lit - Hernández	28
Firelight Praise	28
Freedom come	65
From this house	66
Get up, children!	74
Gloria, hallelujah	37
God bless every step	58
God is a pure no--thing	27
God Was There	81
God, your people seek shelter	62
Good Lord, in that heaven	36
Goodness of sea be thine	75
Hear my cry, O Lord!	51
Holy, holy, holy Lord - Blomquist	83
Holy, holy, holy Lord - Haskel	40
Holy, holy, holy Lord - Haskel	42
Holy, holy, holy Lord - Robinson	4
Hosanna	50
Hosanna	53
Hosanna in Canon	53
Hosanna, ho!	67
I am giving thee worship	70
I am the Spirit's Beloved	52
I am thirsty	35
I asked Lord Jesus	24
I will sing a song of mercy	80
I will supply your need	71
If in your heart	29
If in your heart	30
I'm walking with my God today	11
In God's image I was created	18
Incline your ear	68
Jesu, Jesu, Jesu	22
Justice is moving	73
Kol hanneshama	25
Kyrie eleison	38
Kyrie eleison	39
Kyrie on Five Notes	39
Lamb of God	6
Let my prayer be set forth	16
Let the broken ones be healed	14
Lift up your heads	1
Lord, have mercy	23
Love your enemies	20
Make a noise!	82
Memorial Acclamation - McClellan	5

Memorial Acclamation on Six Notes	43
Mercer Kyrie eleison	38
Mercer Memorial Acclamation	41
Mercer Sanctus	40
My soul is a river	72
Now daylight fades	33
O gracious light - McClellan	3
O gracious light - Scott	47
O send your light forth	9
Offer to God a sacrifice	17
Open my heart	31
Open my heart to your light	60
Our Father in heaven - Dole	85
Our Father in heaven - Haskel	44
Our Father in heaven - Robinson	8
Out of Zion	79
Palm Sunday Processional	67
Peace, perfect peace	7
Phos Hilaron - Robinson	3
Phos Hilaron - Scott	47
Phos Hilaron - Scott	48
Procession to the Table	55
Sanctus and Benedictus - Blomquist	83
Sanctus and Benedictus - Robinson	4
Sanctus on Six Notes	42
Sing praise to God	76
Song of Praise	76
Spirits rising	84
Tar a thighearna tar a thi	63
The bread which we break	45
The earth is the Lord's	55
The Great Entrance	78
The groaning of the Spirit	19
The Lord's Prayer - Dole	85
The Lord's Prayer - Robinson	8
This is the true bread	46
To the bath and the table	56
Walking with my God today	11
We are walking	64
We praise you, we bless you	41
When I was in trouble	81
Where I go in the world	32
Who Is This King?	1
You have grounded my soul	13
Yours is the day	26